FIRST DICTIONARY

Author
Martin Manser

Designer
Angela Ashton

Editor
Sue Churchill

Project Management
Sarah Eason

Editorial Assistance
Liz Dalby and Helen Parker

Artwork Commissioning
Susanne Grant and Lynne French

Production
Jenni Cozens and Ian Paulyn

Art Director
Clare Sleven

Editorial Director
Paula Borton

Director
Jim Miles

ISBN 0-439-22711-9

Published by Scholastic Inc., 555 Broadway, New York, NY 10012,
by arrangement with Chancellor Press, an imprint of Bounty Books,
a division of the Octopus Publishing Group Ltd.

12 11 10 9 8 7 6 5 4 3 2 1 0 1 2 3 4 5/0

Printed in the U.S.A. 14

First Scholastic printing, September 2000

Originally published as *First Dictionary*

FIRST DICTIONARY

SCHOLASTIC INC.
New York Toronto London Auckland Sydney
Mexico City New Delhi Hong Kong

How to use your dictionary

A dictionary is a book of words

Everyone who has helped to make this book hopes that you will find it clear and useful.

You can use a dictionary to see:

- how words are spelt
- what words mean
- how words are used

Many of the words have pictures that help to show what the words mean.

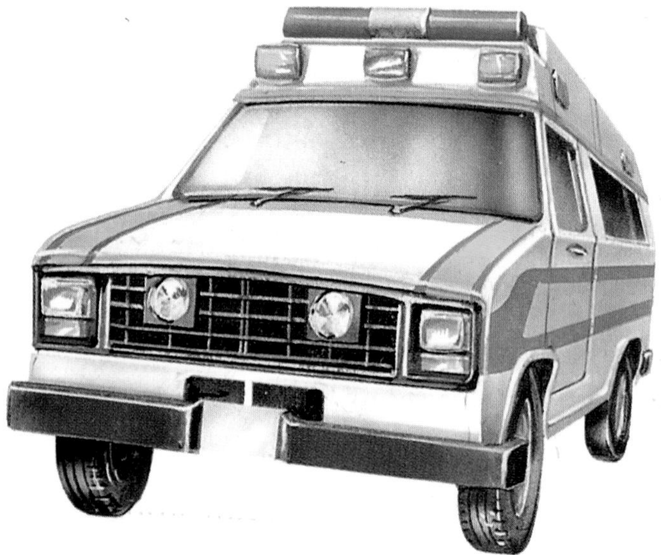

The alphabet

A dictionary is a list of words in alphabetical order. This is the alphabet:

ABCDEFGHIJKLMNOPQRSTUVWXYZ

Words that begin with A come before those beginning with B. Words that begin with B come before those beginning with C, and so on.

In each letter, the words are listed in alphabetical order. For example:

care

careful

careless

carpet

Spelling

Some letters in the spelling of a word are silent. This means that they are used in the spelling but you don't say them. For example:

hour, where we don't say the h

write, where we don't say the w

Grammar

After the main entry word we tell you about the grammar of the word. To make this dictionary easy to use, we only show noun, verb and adjective:

crawl VERB

crayon NOUN

crooked ADJECTIVE

If a word can be used in more than one grammatical way, then the main entry word is repeated:

drill NOUN a tool for making holes in things.

drill VERB to make a hole in something.

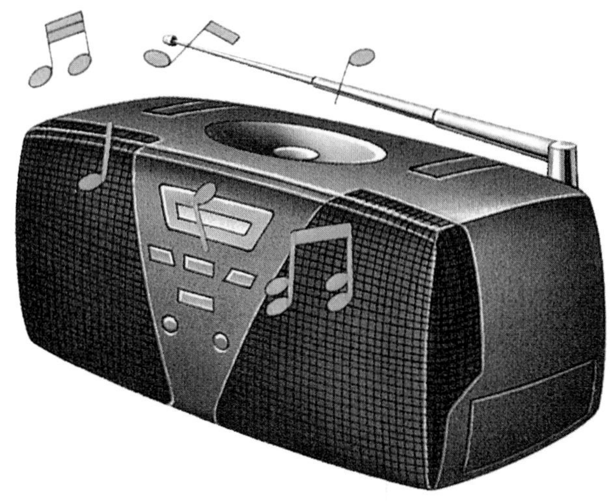

After the main entry word, for some words we tell you more about their grammar:

calf NOUN (PLURAL calves)

big ADJECTIVE (bigger, biggest)

bite VERB (biting, bit, bitten)

Definitions

The main part of the dictionary entry is the definition. This gives you the meaning of the word. For example:

microscope NOUN an instrument that you look through which makes very small objects appear bigger.

If the word has more than one meaning, then these are separated by numbers:

sponge NOUN **1** something you wash with that soaks up water. **2** a light cake.

Examples

These show you how to use many of the words. They are written in *italic* in the text.

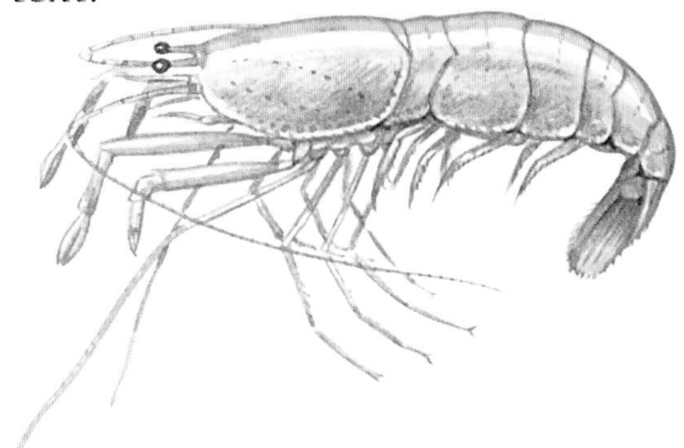

Finding out about words

Some entries have the word *See.* This tells you to go to a particular word to find out more about it:

bought *See* **buy**. *We bought a new car yesterday.*

This means that you should look at the word **buy** to find out more about the word **bought**.

We have also included many words that we use to talk about language. Examples are:

adjective, adverb, comma, full stop, noun, synonym and verb.

Aa

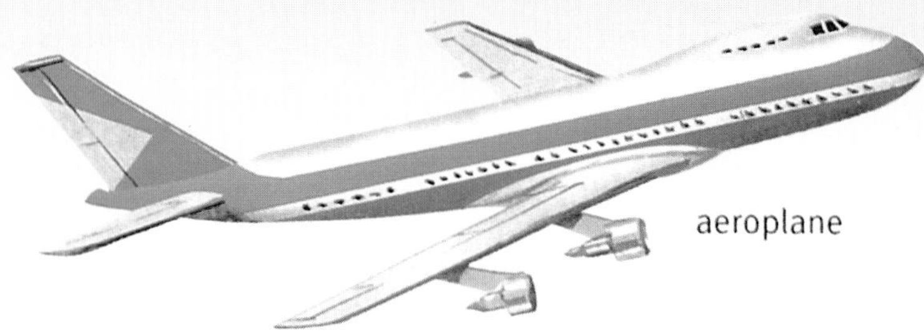

aeroplane

a, an one. *A dog. An egg.*

about on the subject of. *We talked about our holiday.*

above higher than. *The picture is above the television.*

abroad to a foreign country.

absent ADJECTIVE not here, not present. *Jason is absent today because he is ill.*

accident NOUN something, especially something bad, that happens by chance.

accident

ache VERB (aching, ached) to feel a pain for a long time. *My legs ache.*

acorn NOUN the nut that is the fruit of an oak tree. *The huge oak grew from a tiny acorn.*

acrobat NOUN a person who is skilled at walking along high wires or at doing difficult jumps. *The acrobats put on a breathtaking display.*

across from one side of something to the other. *Walk across a road.*

did you know?

adjective

- An *adjective* is a word that tells us about a noun.

  In *'a small car'*, *'small'* is an adjective that describes *'car'*.

adverb

- An *adverb* is a word that tells us when, where, how or why something happens.

  In '*yesterday it was snowing heavily*', '*yesterday*' and '*heavily*' are adverbs. They say when and how it was snowing.
- We often make an adverb by adding '*–ly*' to the end of an adjective. For example, *bad – badly. Great – greatly.*

act VERB **1** to play a part in a play or film. **2** to behave.

active ADJECTIVE moving about, busy, energetic.

acorn

actor NOUN a person who plays a part in a play or film. *The film we saw on TV had a really good actor in it.*

add VERB to put something together with another thing. *If you add 2 and 3 you get 5.*

address NOUN (plural addresses) the number or name of your house, the name of your road and the town where you live. *My address is 87 East Street, Winchester.*

address

adult NOUN a person who is grown up, not a child.

adventure NOUN an activity that is unusual and exciting. *Ali's first trip in an aeroplane was quite an adventure.*

advertisement NOUN an announcement telling you about something that people want to sell you. You can see advertisements on television, in newspapers and on big hoardings in the streets.

aeroplane NOUN a vehicle with wings and engines that flies through the air.

afraid ADJECTIVE **1** frightened because you think something bad is going to happen. **2** sorry. *I'm afraid I've broken it.*

after following in time or order. *After lunch.*

afternoon NOUN the part of the day between lunchtime and evening.

again one more time. *You're becoming better at playing that piece of music – but try it again.*

against 1 touching, next to. *Against the wall.* **2** on the opposite side of. *United are playing against Liverpool.*

age NOUN the number of years that you have lived.

ago before now. *Two days ago.*

agree VERB to think in the same way as someone else. *I agree with Lucy.*

ahead in front of you, in a forward position. *Walk straight ahead.*

air NOUN the mixture of gases that are around the earth and that we breathe. *We went for a walk in the fresh air.*

aircraft NOUN a flying vehicle with wings and engines. Aeroplanes, gliders and helicopters are all different kinds of aircraft.

airport NOUN a place where aircraft take off and land.

ajar ADJECTIVE slightly open. *The door was ajar.*

alarm

alarm NOUN **1** a bell or flashing light that gives a warning of danger. **2** a sudden feeling of fear.

alarm clock NOUN a clock you can set so it rings to wake you up at a certain time.

alike ADJECTIVE similar. *The twins look alike.*

alive ADJECTIVE living.

all the whole of a group or thing. *All the children were very excited.*

alley NOUN a narrow path or street.

alligator NOUN a large dangerous animal that is similar to a crocodile.

ajar

did you know?

alphabet

- The *alphabet* is the set of letters that we arrange in a particular order when we write words.
- The letters of the alphabet are:

  A B C D E F G H I J K L M N O P Q R S T U V W X Y Z.
- We use the alphabetical order of letters to help us find words in books such as dictionaries or in lists.

alligator

allow VERB to let someone do or have something.

almost very nearly. *Emma is almost one metre tall.*

alone ADJECTIVE not with other people.

along from one end of something to the other. *Walk along the road.*

aloud so that people can hear you.

already before now. *I've already eaten my tea.*

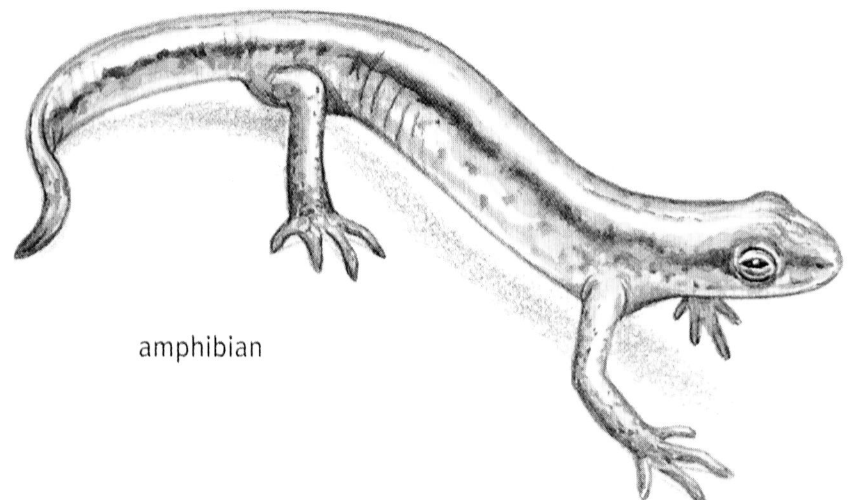

amphibian

also as well, too. *Three hamsters and also two rabbits.*

although even though. *Although it had started to rain, we still went for a picnic.*

altogether 1 completely. *This new music is altogether different.* **2** as a total. *Thirty matches altogether.*

always at all times.

am *See* **be**. *I am six years old.*

amazing ADJECTIVE very surprising and pleasing.

ambulance NOUN a vehicle for carrying people who are ill or injured to and from hospital.

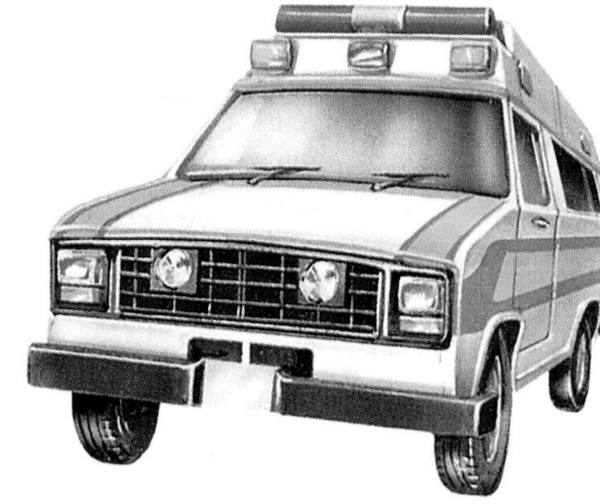

ambulance

amount NOUN how much there is of something. *A large amount of money.*

amphibian NOUN an animal that can live on land and in water. *Frogs are amphibians.*

an *See* **a**.

and used to join two or more words or groups of words. *Mum and Dad.*

angle NOUN a corner where two lines or surfaces meet.

angry ADJECTIVE (angrier, angriest) having a strong feeling about something that you think is bad or unfair.

animal NOUN a living creature, such as a cat, rabbit or tiger.

ankle NOUN the part of your body where your foot joins your leg.

annoy VERB to make someone feel angry and impatient. *It annoys me when my sister leaves her clothes lying all over the floor in our bedroom.*

another one more of the same kind. *Another drink.*

answer VERB to say something back to someone who has just asked you something. *He asked me a question and I answered him.*

did you know?

antonym

- An *antonym* is a word that has a meaning that is opposite to another word: '*slow*' is the antonym of '*fast*'; '*sad*' is the antonym of '*happy*'.

answer NOUN **1** what you say or write when you answer a question. **2** something that is given as a result of thinking. *The answer to a maths question.*

ant NOUN a small crawling insect that lives in a large group of similar creatures.

ant

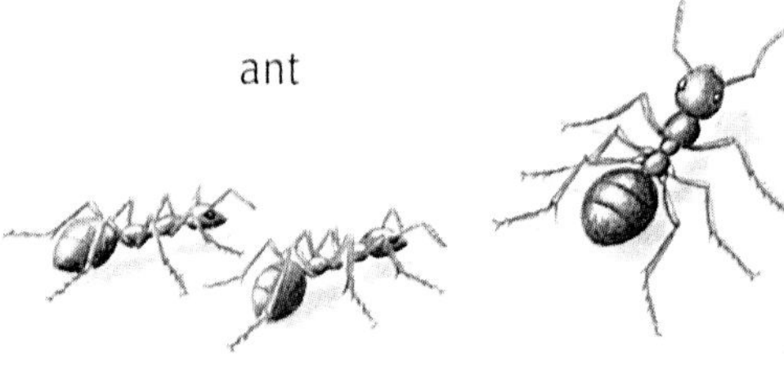

did you know?

apostrophe

- We call the mark (') an *apostrophe*.
- Apostrophes are used in two different ways:
  1 to show that something belongs to someone: '*Tracy's doll*' is a way of saying that the doll belongs to Tracy. Other examples: *A cat's whiskers. Animals' tails. Children's games.*
  2 to show that one or more letters have been left out; for example: *don't = do not* (the 'o' has been left out). Other examples: *Can't = cannot. Didn't = did not. Hasn't = has not. I'll = I will. It's = it is. You're = you are.*

any 1 some of a particular thing. *I don't want to have any chocolate, thanks.* **2** no matter what, who or which kind. *Any size box will do.*

apart at a distance from someone or something. *With his feet apart.*

ape NOUN an animal related to a monkey, with a little or no tail.

appear VERB **1** to come into sight. *Tim suddenly appeared from behind a tree.* **2** to look, to seem.

April

apple NOUN a round fruit that grows on a tree, with a smooth, red, green or yellow skin. *'Would you like another apple?' asked Miriam.*

April NOUN the fourth month of the year, after March and before May. *Last April it rained almost every day.*

apron NOUN a piece of clothing that you wear in front of your normal clothes to stop them from getting dirty. *'Quick, put an apron on before you get paint all over your shirt,' said Carol, crossly.*

aquarium NOUN (plural aquaria or aquariums) a glass or plastic tank that is filled with water and in which you keep fish.

aquarium

are *See* **be**. *'You are my best friend,' Sally told Sandra.*

aren't = are not. *'You're coming to our home, aren't you?' Callum asked Luke.*

area NOUN **1** a particular part of a city, country, etc. **2** the measure of a surface. *The area of a rectangle is its length multiplied by its width.*

argue VERB (arguing, argued) to disagree with someone, often in an angry way.

arithmetic NOUN adding, subtracting, multiplying and dividing numbers.

arm NOUN one of the two parts of your body that come from your shoulders. *Your hands are at the ends of your arms.*

around situated on every side of something. *A fence around the playground.*

arrive VERB (arriving, arrived) to reach a place, especially at the end of a journey. *Arrive home.*

arrow NOUN a long thin weapon with a sharp point at one end. *Arrows are shot from a bow.*

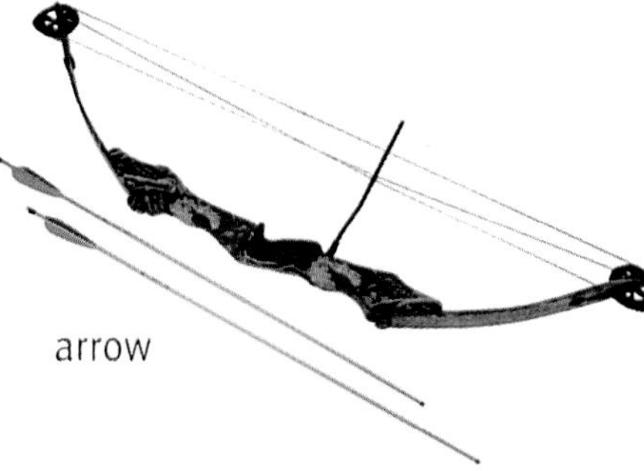

arrow

art NOUN the making of paintings, drawings and sculptures. *My favourite subject at school is art.*

artist NOUN a person who draws, paints or makes other works of art.

as 1 used in comparing things. *As green as grass.* **2** for the reason that, because. *I bought my own diary, as I didn't want to keep borrowing Jack's.*

ask VERB to say something to someone as a question, in order to find out some information. *'What time is the train?' asked Kirsty.*

asleep

asleep ADJECTIVE (sleeping). When you are asleep, you are sleeping. *I was asleep in bed when the telephone rang.*

assembly NOUN (plural assemblies) a group of people who meet together. *School assembly.*

astronaut

astronaut NOUN a person who travels into space in a spacecraft.

at used to show where something is. *At home.*

ate *See* **eat**. *At lunchtime, I ate my sandwiches and a delicious apple.*

atlas NOUN (plural atlases) a book of maps.

attack VERB to be violent towards someone, to hurt someone.

attention NOUN looking at, listening to or thinking about something carefully. *I gave my homework my full attention.*

attic NOUN a room at the top of a house, just below the roof.

August

attract VERB **1** to cause to like or admire. **2** to cause to come to something. *Magnets attract iron.*

audience NOUN the people who watch or listen to a play, film or television programme.

August NOUN the eighth month of the year, after July and before September.

aunt NOUN the sister of your mother or father.

author NOUN the person who writes a book, play, etc.

automatic ADJECTIVE able to work without human help.

autumn NOUN the season in the year between summer and winter. *In autumn, the leaves fall off the trees.*

autumn

did you know?

author

Robert Louis Stevenson was a Scottish author who wrote romantic adventure stories such as *Treasure Island.*

He lived with his family on the island of Samoa, in the South Seas, where he died in 1894.

awake ADJECTIVE not asleep, not sleeping.

awake

away from one place to another place. *We moved away from Chester to Scotland.*

axe NOUN a tool that has a blade at the end of a long handle and is used for cutting wood.

Bb

bag

baby

baby NOUN (PLURAL babies) a very young child that cannot yet talk or walk.

back NOUN **1** the part of your body that is behind you, from your neck to your hips. **2** the part of something that is furthest from the front. *At the back of the room.*

back in the direction that is opposite to the one in which you are facing or where you are. *Mum is driving the car back.*

backwards the direction that is opposite to the one you are facing.

bacon NOUN meat from the back or sides of a pig that is salted or smoked.

bad ADJECTIVE not good, not pleasant. *Bad weather.*

badge NOUN a small piece of metal or cloth you fix to your clothes to show who you are, what you do or what you have done.

badger NOUN a wild animal that lives underground and has a white head and two wide black stripes on it.

bag NOUN a container made of paper, plastic or leather that has an opening at the top and that you use to carry things.

bake VERB (baking, baked) to cook food in an oven.

baked beans PLURAL NOUN beans that are cooked in tomato sauce.

baker NOUN **1** a person whose job is to bake and sell bread and cakes. **2** a shop where you can buy bread and cakes.

baker

balance NOUN steadiness. *Adam lost his balance.*

balance VERB (balancing, balanced) to keep yourself or something steady without falling over.

bald ADJECTIVE having little or no hair on your head. *Graham's father is going bald.*

ball NOUN a round object that is used in games such as football, cricket and tennis. *He caught the ball.*

ballet NOUN a kind of dancing performed by dancers who make carefully planned movements, usually to music.

balloon

balloon NOUN a thin rubber bag which you blow air into so that it becomes larger and goes up in the air. *Coloured balloons at our birthday party.*

A B C D E F G H I J K L M N O P Q R S T U V W X Y Z

banana NOUN a long curved fruit with a yellow skin which you peel off to eat the inside.

band NOUN **1** a group of musicians. **2** a flat narrow strip of cloth that you wear around your head or wrists.

bandage NOUN a long strip of cloth to wrap round a wound.

bang NOUN a sudden loud noise, an explosion.

bang

bank NOUN **1** a place where your money is kept safely. **2** the raised side along the edge of a river or lake.

bar NOUN **1** a long straight piece of metal. **2** a roughly rectangular piece of solid material. *A bar of chocolate.* **3** a place where you can buy a drink.

barber NOUN a person who cuts men's hair.

bare ADJECTIVE not covered by clothing.

bark VERB to make a short loud noise.

baseball NOUN a game played with a bat and a ball and two teams of nine players.

bananas

basin NOUN **1** a bowl which you use to wash your hands and face. **2** a bowl used for mixing or storing food.

basket NOUN a container made of straw or thin sticks that have been woven together.

basketball NOUN a game in which two teams of five players try to score a goal by throwing a large ball through a circular net at each end of the court.

bat NOUN **1** a specially shaped piece of wood used in some games to hit a ball. **2** a small flying animal which comes out at night and looks like a mouse.

bath NOUN a long large container for water that you sit in to wash your whole body.

did you know?

beak

The hummingbird uses its beak to probe for nectar, the crossbill cracks seeds with its beak, and the golden eagle uses its beak to tear flesh.

bathe VERB (bathing, bathed) to swim.

bathroom NOUN a room in a house with a bath or shower, a basin and often a toilet.

battery NOUN (PLURAL batteries) a container that produces electricity to be used in something such as a clock, torch or radio.

battle NOUN a fight between enemies.

be VERB (am, are, is, being, was, were, been) **1** to exist. **2** to become. **3** to take place.

beach NOUN (PLURAL beaches) an area of land by the sea, covered with sand or small stones. *On sunny days, Mary liked to go to the beach.*

bead NOUN a small piece of coloured glass, wood or plastic used as jewellery or decoration and which has a hole through the middle through which you thread a string or wire.

beak

beak NOUN the hard curved or pointed part of the mouth of a bird. *The bird carried twigs for its nest in its beak.*

bean NOUN the seed of a climbing plant that is eaten as a vegetable. *Runner beans are my favourite kind of vegetable.*

bear

bear NOUN a large strong wild animal that is covered with thick rough fur.

beard NOUN the hair that grows on a man's chin and cheeks.

beat VERB (beat, beaten) **1** to hit someone or something very hard. **2** to do better than another person or team in a race or competition. **3** to move regularly. *Can you hear your heart beating?*

beaten *See* **beat**. *Our team has beaten your team.*

beautiful ADJECTIVE very attractive, very pleasing.

became *See* **become**. *The smell became stronger.*

because for the reason that. *I can't come to your party because I am ill.*

become VERB (becoming, became, become) to come to be.

bed NOUN the piece of furniture that you lie down to sleep on.

bedroom NOUN the room in your house which is used for sleeping in.

bee NOUN an insect with a yellow and black striped body that makes honey and can sting you painfully.

bee

beef NOUN the meat of farm cattle such as a cow or bull.

been VERB *See* **be**. *It has been a lovely day.*

beer NOUN an alcoholic drink made from grain and hops.

beetle NOUN an insect that has hard wing coverings.

before earlier than. *Before eleven o'clock.*

did you know?

bear

There are eight species of bear. The polar bear, which lives in the Arctic, is the biggest of all bears. Fully grown males can grow up to 2.6m.
The sunbear that lives in the jungles of Southeast Asia, is the smallest bear. They are said to weigh no more than 65kg.

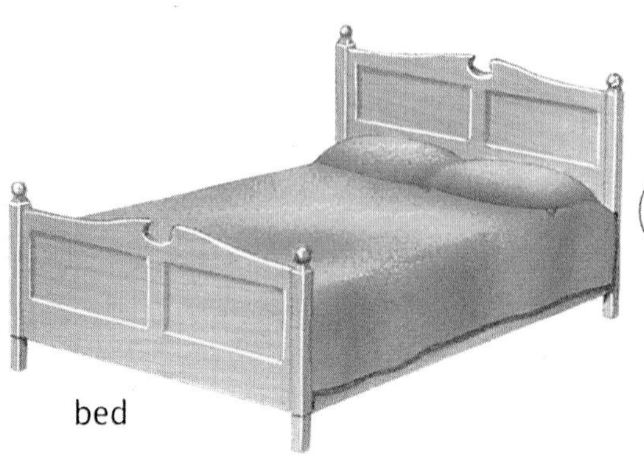
bed

began *See* **begin**. *Sarah began to laugh loudly.*

begin VERB (beginning, began, begun) to start to do something.

begun *See* **begin**. *Has school begun yet?*

behave VERB (behaving, behaved) to act. *You should behave nicely.*

behind facing the back of something or someone. *Hide behind the door.*

being *See* **be**. *You're being silly.*

being NOUN a living thing, especially a person. *A human being.*

believe VERB (believing, believed) to think that something is true.

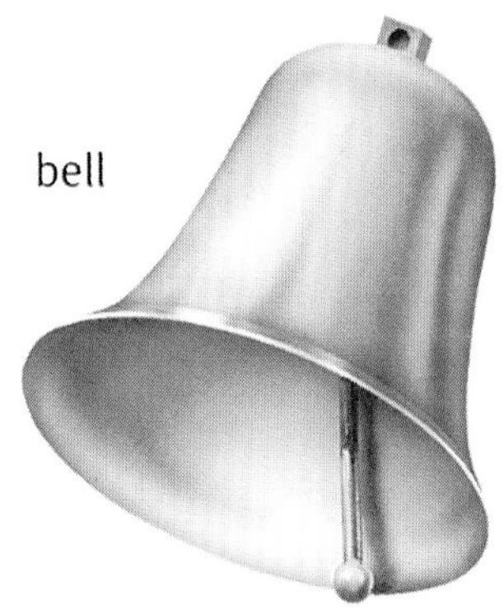
bell

bell NOUN **1** a hollow metal object that makes a ringing sound when you hit it.
2 a device that makes a ringing sound.

A **B** C D E F G H I J K L M N O P Q R S T U V W X Y Z

belong VERB to be owned by. *This book belongs to Emma Peters.*

below in a lower position than something else. *Below the ceiling.*

belt NOUN a strip of cloth or leather that you fasten round your waist.

bench NOUN a long seat for two or more people.

bend NOUN the curved part of a road or river.

bend VERB (bent) to make something straight become curved. *Bend your leg.*

bent *See* **bend**. *He bent the fork.*

berry NOUN (PLURAL berries) a small soft round fruit.

beside

beside at the side of or next to something. *Sit beside me.*

best ADJECTIVE *The best book that I have ever read.*

better ADJECTIVE *Fruit is better for you than crisps.*

bicycle

between having one person or thing on one side and another person or thing on the other side. *James is sitting between Luke and Tom.*

bicycle NOUN a vehicle which has two wheels and which you pedal with your feet.

berries

big ADJECTIVE (bigger, biggest) large in size, importance, etc.

bike *See* **bicycle**.

bikini NOUN a two-piece swimming costume that women and girls wear.

binoculars PLURAL NOUN a pair of special glasses that you look through to see things that are a long way away.

bird NOUN a creature that has feathers and wings and lays eggs. Most birds can fly.

birthday NOUN the day on which you were born.

biscuit NOUN a small flat cake that is crisp and sweet.

bit NOUN a small piece or amount of something.

bit *See* **bite**. *I bit into the cake.*

bite VERB (biting, bit, bitten) to use your teeth to cut into something.

bitten *See* **bite**. *Have you ever been bitten by a dog?*

bitter ADJECTIVE **1** having a sharp and unpleasant taste. **2** feeling angry and sad.

black ADJECTIVE the darkest colour, the colour of coal.

blackbird NOUN a common bird that has black or brown feathers.

did you know?

bird

There are more than 9,000 different kinds of birds in the world. The ostrich is the largest living bird, standing more than 2m high, and possibly weighing twice as much as a man.

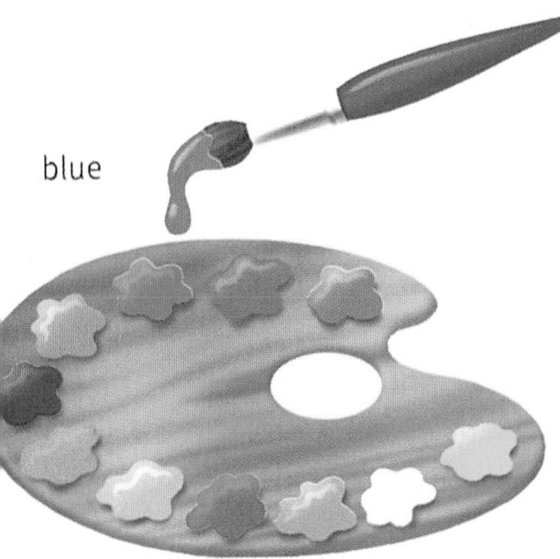

blue

blackboard NOUN a dark-coloured board with a smooth surface that teachers write on with chalk.

blame NOUN the responsibility for causing or doing something bad.

blame VERB (blaming, blamed) to think or say that someone is responsible for something.

blanket NOUN a large piece of thick material used as a cover on a bed to keep you warm.

blew *See* **blow**. *Warm air blew in through the window.*

blind ADJECTIVE not able to see.

blink VERB to shut your eyes and open them again quickly.

block NOUN **1** a large piece of wood, stone, etc. **2** a large building of flats or offices. *We live in a block of flats in the city.*

block VERB to prevent movement. *When the lorry broke down it blocked the road and none of the cars could pass.*

blood NOUN the red liquid that flows inside the veins in your body. Blood is pumped round the body by the heart.

blouse NOUN a piece of clothing for girls and women that reaches from the neck to the waist.

blow VERB (blew, blown) to make the air move, to move with the air.

blown *See* **blow**. *The tree was blown down in the storm.*

blue ADJECTIVE having the colour of the sky on a sunny day.

blunt ADJECTIVE **1** having a rounded or flat end, not sharp. **2** speaking in a plain way, without wanting to be polite.

board NOUN a flat piece of wood or other material.

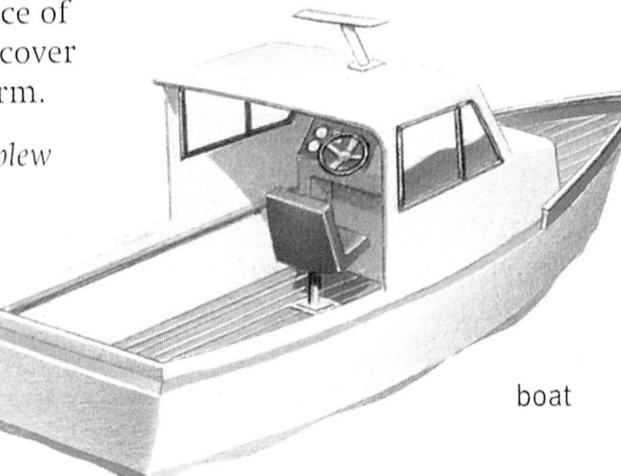

boat

did you know?

blood

Blood is made up of red and white blood cells. Red blood cells carry oxygen around the body, to our muscles, heart, lungs and other important organs. Our white blood cells fight harmful bacteria.

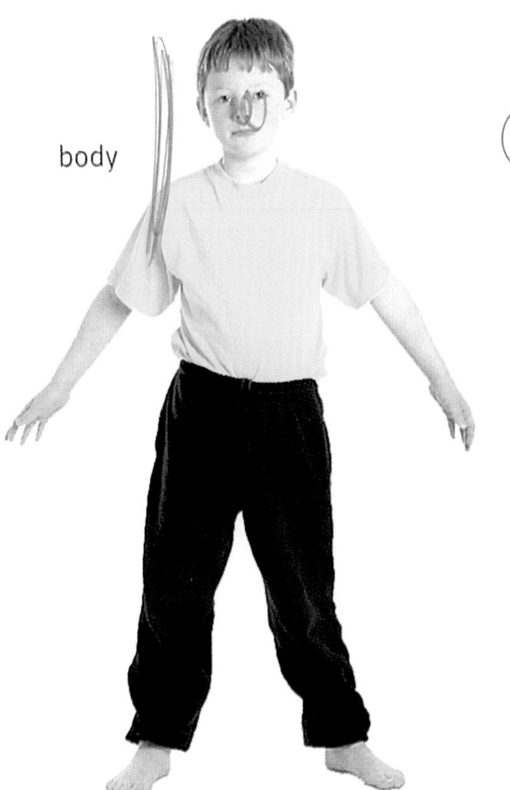

body

boat NOUN a small ship. There are many different kinds of boat, such as canoes and sailing boats.

body NOUN (PLURAL bodies) **1** all of a person, including their head, arms and legs. **2** the main part of a person, excluding their head, arms and legs. **3** a dead person.

boil VERB **1** to make liquid hot so that bubbles appear on it and it starts to change into steam. **2** to cook food in boiling water.

boiler NOUN a device that burns gas, oil, etc., to produce hot water.

bomb NOUN a device that is filled with materials that will make it explode.

bone NOUN one of the hard white parts under the skin of your body.

bonfire

bonfire NOUN a large fire outside, often used to burn rubbish.

book NOUN a collection of printed pages fastened together for reading.

bookshop NOUN a shop that sells books.

boot NOUN a shoe that covers your foot and the lower part of your leg.

bored ADJECTIVE not interested, tired of something. *Andrew was bored of doing his homework.*

boring ADJECTIVE dull and not interesting.

born VERB (be born) to start your life. *I was born in 1991.*

did you know?

brain

In some small insects the brain is no bigger than a speck of dust. Mammals, however, have big brains in relation to their size. Human brains are the biggest of all.

borrow VERB to take something which belongs to someone else, usually with their permission, and which you are going to give them back later.

both two people or things.

bottle NOUN a container made of plastic or glass that you keep liquids in.

bottom NOUN the lowest part of something.

bought *See* **buy**. *We bought a new car yesterday.*

bounce VERB (bouncing, bounced) to move upwards immediately after hitting a hard surface.

bow (said like **how**) VERB to bend your body or your head to show respect towards someone.

bow (said like **low**) NOUN **1** a knot with two loops. **2** a curved stick that is used for shooting arrows. **3** a long, thin piece of wood with horses' hair stretched on it, used to play a musical instrument such as a violin.

bowl NOUN a deep round container used to mix, store or serve food.

box NOUN (PLURAL boxes) a container with stiff sides and often a lid.

box VERB to fight someone by punching with the fists.

boy NOUN a male child.

bra NOUN underwear worn by a woman to support her breasts.

bracelet NOUN a wrist band or ring worn as a decoration.

brackets PLURAL NOUN the marks ( ) that you can put round some words in a sentence. You put them round words that you could leave out and still leave the meaning of the whole sentence clear. For example: *Mrs Green (Samantha's mother) went to see the headteacher.* Brackets are always used as a pair.

box

brain NOUN the part inside your head that you use to think and feel. The brain sends messages to other parts of your body to control them.

break

brake NOUN a device that makes a car, bicycle, etc., go slower or stop.

branch NOUN (PLURAL branches) the part of a tree that grows out from the trunk and has leaves, flowers or fruit growing on it.

branch

brave ADJECTIVE willing to do things that are dangerous or painful, not showing fear, having courage.

bread NOUN a common food made from mixing and then baking flour, water and yeast.

break VERB (broke, broken) **1** to cause to fall into two or more pieces, because it has been hit or dropped. **2** to damage a machine so that it no longer works.

breakfast NOUN the first meal of the day.

breathe VERB (breathing, breathed) to take air into your body and let it out again.

did you know?

breathing

We rarely think about breathing, but we all need the oxygen in air to stay alive. Oxygen is used with food to give our body the energy it needs to work. When we breathe air into our lungs, oxygen passes into the blood stream through tiny air sacs called 'alveoli'. Oxygen is then carried in our blood to all the organs of the body.

brick NOUN a rectangular piece of baked clay used for building.

bridge NOUN a structure that carries a road or railway over a river, valley, etc.

bright ADJECTIVE having a strong, light colour.

brown

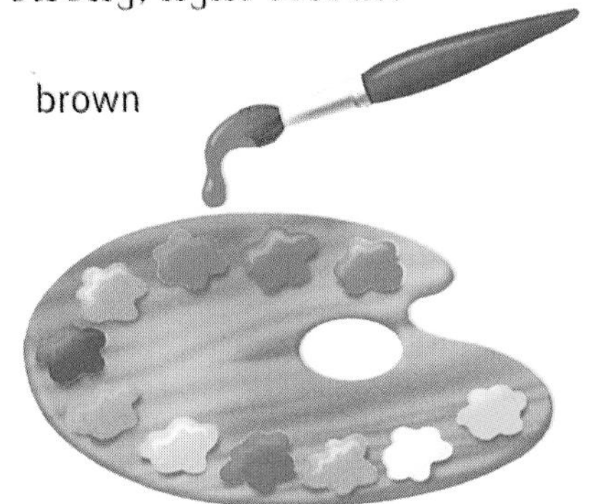

brother

bring VERB (brought) to fetch, carry or take with you.

broke, **broken** *See* **break**. *Lisa broke her arm yesterday. Paul has just broken a window.*

brother NOUN a boy or man who has the same parents as you.

brought *See* **bring**. *I've brought an umbrella with me.*

brown ADJECTIVE having the colour of wood or earth.

brush NOUN (PLURAL brushes) tool for sweeping, smoothing or painting, made of stiff hair or nylon.

brush VERB to clean, smooth or tidy using a brush. *I brushed my hair until it was smooth.*

bubble NOUN a ball of air in a liquid.

A B C D E F G H I J K L M N O P Q R S T U V W X Y Z

bucket NOUN a round metal or plastic container that has a handle and is used to hold or carry water.

bud NOUN a small bump on a tree or plant that grows into a leaf or flower.

bud

bug NOUN an insect. Ants and bees are bugs.

build VERB (built, built) to make something by putting pieces together. *We built a sandcastle on the beach.*

building NOUN a structure with a roof and walls, such as a house, shop or factory.

building

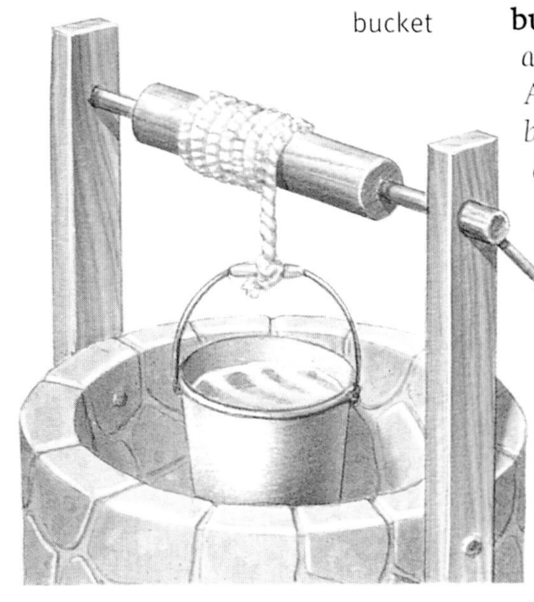

bucket

built *See* **build**. *The house that Jack built.*

bulb NOUN **1** the glass part of an electric lamp that gives out light. **2** a round type of root that grows into a plant. *Daffodils grow from bulbs.*

bull NOUN a male form of cattle or certain other animals. A cow is the female.

bump NOUN **1** a minor car accident when cars hit each other. **2** a round swelling.

bump VERB to hit something accidentally.

bunch NOUN (PLURAL bunches) a group of things or people. A bunch of flowers. *We bought a bunch of bananas, and a bunch of flowers for Grandma.*

bungalow NOUN a house built on one level.

burglar NOUN a thief who breaks into someone's house or office and steals things.

burglar

did you know?

bungalow

The word bungalow, for a house on only one level, comes from the Hindi language. It originally meant 'a house in the Bengal style'.

Today, many older people live in bungalows. There are no stairs inside, so it is easier for them to move around the house.

Other words from Hindi that have become part of the English language include: *bangle, chintz, chutney, cot, dinghy, dungarees, gymkhana, juggernaut, jungle, kedgeree, loot, pundit, shampoo, thug, tom-tom.*

burn VERB (burnt or burned) **1** to be on fire. **2** to destroy or damage by fire.

burnt or **burned** See **burn**. *The factory was burnt down.*

burst VERB (burst, burst) to split open suddenly because of the pressure from inside. *The balloon burst with a bang.*

bury VERB (burying, buried) to put the body of a dead person into the ground.

bus NOUN (PLURAL buses) a large motor vehicle for carrying passengers. *Karen ran to catch the bus.*

bush NOUN (PLURAL bushes) a small tree that does not grow very high.

busy ADJECTIVE (busier, busiest) working hard, having many things to do, not free to do something.

butterfly

but 1 used to show a contrast with what has just been said. *I would like to come but I'm on holiday.* **2** except. *She thanked everyone but herself.*

buttons

butcher NOUN a shopkeeper who sells meat.

butler NOUN the chief male servant in a grand house.

butt VERB to push or hit with the head or horns like a bull or goat, to ram.

butter NOUN a yellow fat which you spread on bread.

buttercup NOUN a small plant with yellow petals that grows in fields.

did you know?

butterfly

There are many different kinds of butterflies around the world.

One of the smallest is called the 'Dwarf Blue'. It lives in South Africa and has a wingspan of only one centimetre.

butterfly NOUN (PLURAL butterflies) an insect with large colourful wings. Butterflies grow from caterpillars.

button NOUN a small round object attached to a piece of clothing and used as a fastener.

buttress NOUN a support for an outside wall, most common in old buildings.

buy VERB (bought, bought) to get something by paying money for it. *Mum bought me a new shirt and some new shoes for school when we went shopping.*

buzz NOUN (PLURAL buzzes) a low continuous noise like the sound of a bee.

buzz

buzzard NOUN a large bird of prey that hunts other creatures for food.

by 1 used to show the person or thing that has done something. *A play by Shakespeare.* **2** beside. *A seat by the river.* **3** before. *By Thursday.*

Cc

camel

cabbage NOUN a green vegetable that can be eaten raw or cooked.

cabbage

café NOUN a shop with tables and chairs where you can buy and have drinks and snacks.

cage

cage NOUN a structure of bars in which birds or animals are kept.

cake NOUN a mixture of butter, sugar, eggs, flour and other ingredients that is baked before it is eaten.

calculator NOUN an electronic machine that works out mathematical calculations.

calendar NOUN a list of the days, weeks and months of the year.

calf NOUN (PLURAL calves) **1** the young of some animals, especially the cow, elephant or whale. **2** the back of your leg from the ankle to the knee.

call VERB **1** to shout or cry out. *I heard a voice calling in the night.* **2** to visit briefly. *I'll call for you on my way to school.* **3** to telephone. *Call me tomorrow.* **4** to name. *I am called Mark.*

calm ADJECTIVE peaceful, quiet, still.

calves *See* **calf**.

came *See* **come**. *We came home late from school.*

did you know?

capital letters

Capital letters are used:

1 to begin the first word of a sentence. *This is my book.*
2 to begin a proper noun (see noun). *London is the capital of the United Kingdom.*
3 to begin the days of the week, months and special holidays. *On Monday 3 May. Easter Day.*
4 to begin the first word of a spoken sentence. *'You can go now,' she said.*
5 for the word *I*.
6 for titles of people and organizations. *Dr Patel; Independent Television News.*

camel NOUN an animal with one or two humps that is used for carrying people and goods in the desert.

camera NOUN a piece of equipment used for filming or taking photographs.

camp NOUN a place where people live in tents or huts for a short time, especially on holiday.

camp

camp VERB to live in a tent for a short time.

can NOUN a metal tin or container that is used to keep food or drinks fresh.

can VERB (could) to be able to do something. *I can play the guitar.*

can't = cannot. *I can't read music.*

canal NOUN an artifical waterway made so boats can transport heavy goods.

canary NOUN (PLURAL canaries) a small yellow bird.

candle NOUN a wax stick with a string through the middle which burns to give light.

cannot = can not. *I cannot help you any more.*

cap NOUN **1** a soft hat with a peak. **2** a lid or cover for the end of a bottle or tube.

car NOUN a motor vehicle for carrying a few passengers.

car-boot sale NOUN a place where people gather to sell unwanted goods from the backs of their cars.

caravan NOUN a mobile home that can be towed by a car or a horse.

card NOUN **1** stiff paper. **2** a piece of card or plastic made for identification purposes. *Membership card.* **3** a piece of printed card for sending a message to someone. *Birthday card.* **4** a piece of card, part of a pack, with numbers or pictures printed on it for playing a game like snap.

cardboard NOUN thick stiff paper used for making boxes.

cardigan NOUN a knitted woollen garment with sleeves and which fastens down the front.

candle

care NOUN **1** looking after someone. **2** attention.

care VERB (caring, cared) **1** to feel concerned about something. *Joe cares about the environment.* **2** to look after someone. *The children care for their disabled mother.*

careful ADJECTIVE **1** cautious, not taking risks. **2** done with a lot of attention.

careless ADJECTIVE **1** thoughtless, making mistakes because of lack of attention. **2** without any worries.

carpet NOUN a thick covering for a floor or stairs.

carrier bag NOUN a plastic or paper bag used for carrying shopping.

carrot NOUN an orange-coloured vegetable that grows under the ground.

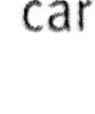
car

did you know?

cardigan

The cardigan is named after the British officer James Thomas Brudenell, 7th Earl of Cardigan (1797–1868). Cardigans were first worn by soldiers in the Crimean War in the 19th century.

carry VERB (carrying, carried) to lift and move something or someone from one place to another.

carry out VERB to fulfil, to do what you have promised or have been told to do.

cart NOUN a vehicle for carrying goods, usually drawn by a horse.

cart VERB to carry something or someone. and find it tiring. *I don't want to cart those bags around town.*

carton NOUN a cardboard box, a container for food or drink. *A carton of juice.*

cardigan

cartoon

cartoon NOUN **1** a funny drawing. **2** an animated film.

case NOUN **1** a box or bag for moving goods. *A packing case.* **2** an example or occurrence of something. *A bad case of flu.* **3** a question to be decided in a lawcourt, with the facts and arguments put forward by each side. *The case was proved.*

cash NOUN money in the form of coins and notes rather than cheques.

cassette NOUN a small plastic container of magnetic tape for recording and playing music, stories, etc.

castle NOUN a large building made strong with high walls and towers.

cat NOUN a small furry animal that has whiskers, a tail and sharp claws and is kept as a pet.

catalogue NOUN a list of the things available from a particular company or organization.

catch VERB (caught, caught) **1** to grasp or capture something. *Catch the ball.* **2** to be in time for. *Catch the train.* **3** to get an illness. *You'll catch a cold if you don't wear a coat.*

did you know?

cartoon

Cartoons were originally rough sketches of the design for a tapestry or painting, they were drawn to the same scale as the finished work. Cartoon films and television programmes have become very popular. They are made by joining together a series of drawings, each one slightly different to the one before. The result is that when these drawings are shown at a very fast speed, it looks as if the scene is moving.

caterpillar NOUN a small worm-like creature that later develops into a butterfly or moth.

cathedral NOUN the main church in an area, a bishop is the church leader in the area.

Catholic NOUN a member of the Roman Catholic Church.

cattle NOUN a collective name for cows, bulls, etc.

caught See **catch**. *Jake caught the ball.*

cauliflower NOUN a vegetable with a white head of flowers.

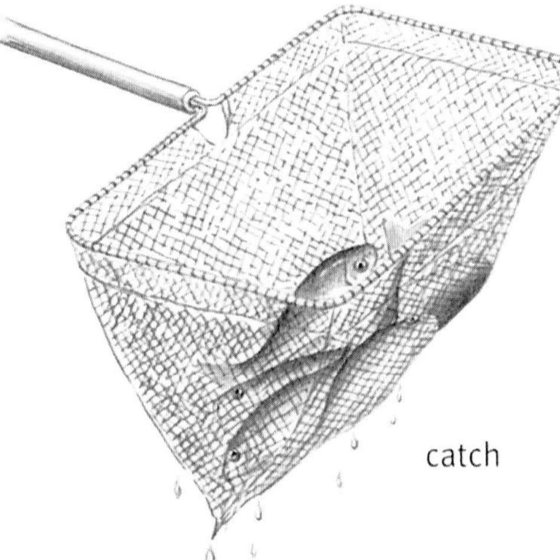
catch

cause NOUN **1** the thing that makes something happen. **2** an aim or purpose that a group of people support.

cause VERB (causing, caused) to make something happen.

cave NOUN a hollow place in the side of a hill or cliff or beneath the ground.

cattle

CD-ROM NOUN a compact disc containing information which can be displayed on a computer screen.

ceiling NOUN the top part of the inside of a room.

centimetre NOUN a measurement equal to 0.01 metres or 0.4 inches.

centre NOUN **1** the middle of something. **2** a building where people take part in different activities or where they go for help. *A sports centre.*

century NOUN (PLURAL centuries) a period of one hundred years.

cereal NOUN **1** grain produced by plants like wheat, barley, oats, etc. **2** a breakfast food that is made from grain.

chain NOUN a length of metal rings that are joined together.

chair NOUN a seat for one person that has a back and can be moved around.

chair

chalk NOUN **1** soft white rock. **2** a piece of this used for writing on a blackboard.

change NOUN **1** something that is different. **2** money given back to you when you pay more than a thing costs.

change VERB (changing, changed) **1** to alter or become different. **2** to replace one thing with another. **3** to put on other clothes.

channel NOUN **1** a narrow stretch of water between two countries or seas. *The English Channel.* **2** a wavelength for broadcasting radio or television programmes.

cereal

chart NOUN a diagram which presents information in a clear, visual way that is easy to understand.

chase VERB (chasing, chased) to run after someone to try to catch them.

cheap ADJECTIVE **1** not expensive, costing very little. **2** of poor quality.

check VERB to make sure something is correct or safe.

cheek NOUN **1** the round part of your face below your eye. **2** rudeness or lack of respect.

cheerful ADJECTIVE happy.

cheese NOUN a solid food that is made from milk.

cherries

cherry NOUN (PLURAL cherries) a small, round fruit with a stone in the middle.

chest NOUN **1** the front part of your body between the stomach and the neck. **2** a strong box. **3** a piece of furniture with drawers.

did you know?

child

If we want to talk about more than one child, we use the plural word *children*.

This is an irregular plural.

Other irregular plurals are: *foot – feet; goose – geese; man – men; mouse – mice; ox – oxen; tooth – teeth; woman – women.*

chew VERB to break up food with your teeth so that it is easier to swallow. *Chew your food thoroughly.*

chicken NOUN **1** a bird kept for its eggs and meat. **2** someone who is a coward.

chickenpox NOUN a disease which gives you a high temperature and itchy red spots. *There was an outbreak of chickenpox at school.*

child NOUN (PLURAL children) a boy or girl who is not yet an adult, someone's son or daughter.

children *See* **child**.

chest

chimney NOUN a narrow opening above a fire that takes smoke out of a building.

chin NOUN the part of your face below the mouth and above the neck.

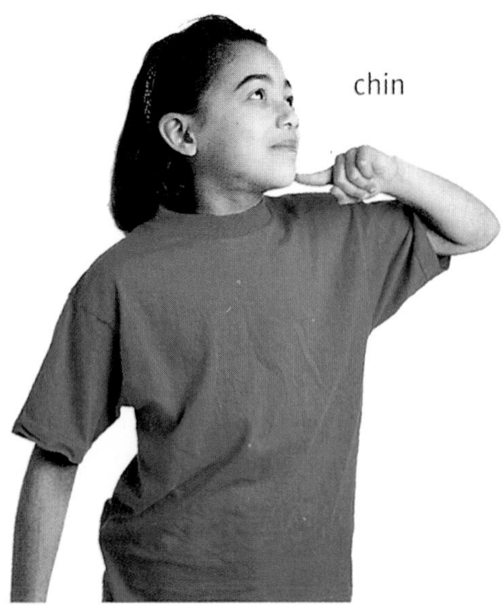

chin

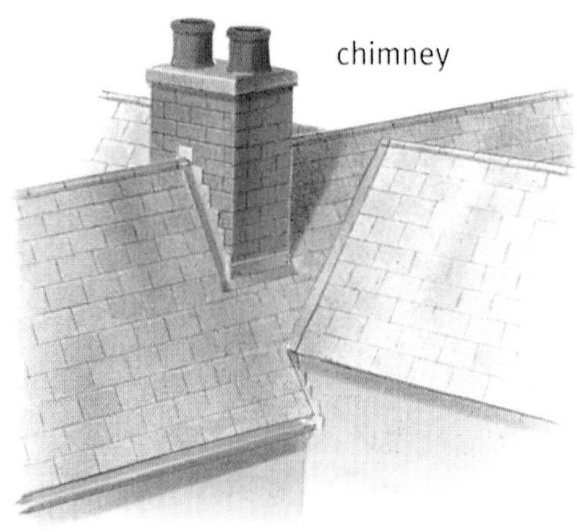

chimney

chips PLURAL NOUN thin pieces of potato that are deep-fried in oil.

chocolate NOUN a sweet or drink made from cocoa beans.

choose VERB (choosing, chose, chosen) to select or pick.

chop VERB (chopping, chopped) to cut up into pieces with an axe or a knife.

chose, chosen *See* **choose**. *I chose a pink dress.*

Christmas NOUN the time of year when the birth of Jesus Christ is celebrated.

Christmas tree NOUN a real or artificial fir tree that is decorated with tinsel and ornaments and people put up in their homes at Christmas.

church NOUN (PLURAL churches) a place of Christian worship. *Sally goes to church every Sunday.*

cigarette NOUN tobacco rolled up in a thin paper tube and smoked. *Smoking cigarettes is bad for your health.*

circle NOUN a perfectly round shape, a ring. *We all sat on the floor in a circle.*

circle

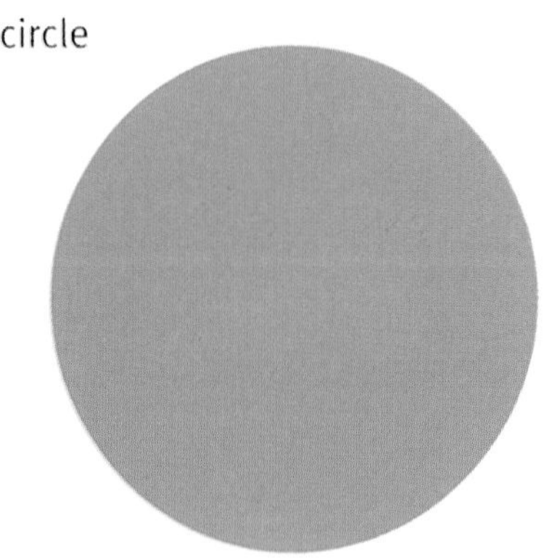

circus NOUN (PLURAL circuses) a show, often in a big tent, given by clowns, acrobats, performing animals, etc. *Every year I look forward to going to the circus.*

city NOUN (PLURAL cities) a large and important town. *The city of London is a centre for financial matters.*

did you know?

chocolate

The word *chocolate* for food made from cacao seeds, derives from the Nahuatl language of Central America.

Other words from Nahuatl that have become part of the English language include: *avocado*, *chilli* and *tomato*.

clap VERB (clapping, clapped) to hit the palms of your hands together to show that you are pleased with something or to get someone's attention.

clarinet

clarinet NOUN a musical instrument with a single reed, played by blowing.

class NOUN (PLURAL classes) a group of children taught together in a school.

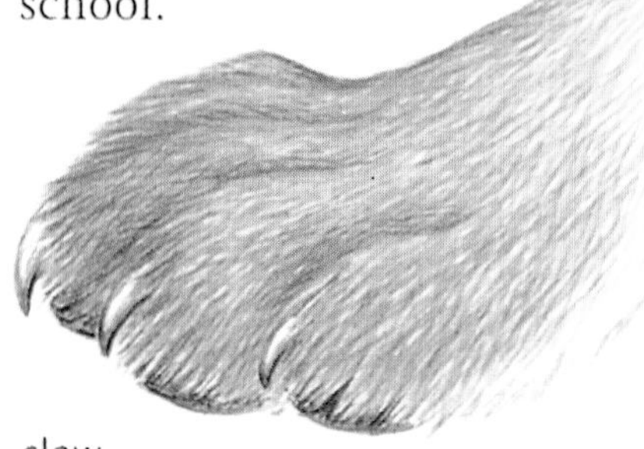

claw

claw NOUN one of the sharp nails on an animal's paw or a bird's foot.

clay NOUN soft, sticky earth that hardens when baked. It is used to make pots and bricks.

clean ADJECTIVE not dirty.

clean VERB to remove dirt and dust from something.

clear ADJECTIVE **1** easy to see through. *Clear glass.* **2** easy to understand. *Clear arguments.* **3** with nothing in the way. *A clear road.*

clear VERB **1** to remove unwanted things from a place. **2** to jump over a fence, wall, etc.

clever ADJECTIVE intelligent, able to learn things easily.

cliff NOUN a high steep piece of land next to the sea.

climb VERB to go up towards the top of something.

climb

cloakroom NOUN **1** a room in which you can leave your coat and bags. *I hung my jacket in the cloakroom.* **2** a room with a toilet and washbasin. *Wash the cloakroom floor.*

did you know?

clothes

We use clothes to protect ourselves, to keep warm and to change the way we look. Clothes were first made from animal skins. Now we can use many different types and colours of fabric to make them.

Styles of clothes change with time, and also change depending on the weather, or what the person wearing them is doing. Clothes can show that we belong to a group, for example a school uniform.

clock NOUN a device for showing the time of day. *Look at the clock and tell me the time.*

close (said like **dose**) ADJECTIVE **1** near. **2** careful. *A close look.*

close (said like **rose**) VERB (closing, closed) to shut.

close-up a photograph or film that is taken from very near.

cloth NOUN **1** woven material used especially to make clothes. **2** a piece of cloth used for a particular purpose. *A dishcloth.*

clothes PLURAL NOUN the garments that people wear. *She needs new clothes.*

cloud NOUN a mass of tiny drops of water, dust or smoke, floating in the air.

clown NOUN someone, often a circus performer, who makes people laugh by doing silly things.

clue NOUN something that helps you to find the answer.

coach NOUN (PLURAL coaches) **1** a bus. **2** a four-wheeled vehicle pulled by horses. **3** a trainer, especially for sports.

coast

coal NOUN a hard, black substance that is mined for burning as a fuel.

coast NOUN land by the sea.

coat NOUN **1** a garment with sleeves worn over other clothes to keep you warm outdoors. **2** an animal's fur. **3** a layer of paint.

coconut NOUN large, hollow nut of a palm tree which contains milky juice and a white lining that you can eat.

coconut

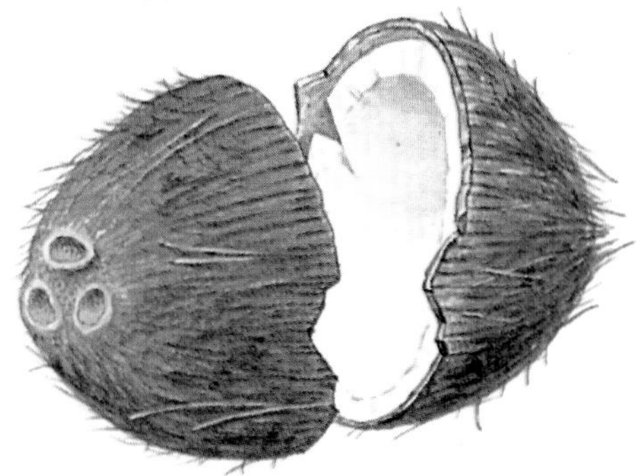

coffee NOUN **1** powder made by roasting and crushing the beans of a plant, used for drinks or as a flavouring. **2** a drink made by mixing boiling water with this powder.

coin NOUN (PLURAL coins) a disc of metal used for money.

coins

cola NOUN fizzy brown drink.

cold ADJECTIVE not warm.

cold NOUN illness that gives you a runny nose and a sore throat.

collar NOUN the part of a shirt or coat that fits round the neck.

collect VERB to gather things together.

comic

college NOUN a place where you can go and do further study after leaving school.

colon The punctuation mark (:) is a colon. It is used to introduce a statement or list. *To bake a cake you will need the following ingredients: flour, sugar, butter, eggs and milk.*

colour NOUN red, blue, green, yellow, etc.

colour VERB to give colour to something with paint, crayons, etc.

colour

comb NOUN a piece of plastic, metal, etc., with teeth for tidying your hair.

comb VERB to tidy your hair with a comb.

come VERB (coming, came, come) **1** to move towards. *Come over here.* **2** to arrive. *Come at four o'clock.* **3** to go with someone. *Come with me.*

comfortable ADJECTIVE **1** making you feel relaxed. **2** not worried, at ease.

comic NOUN **1** a comedian. **2** a children's magazine with cartoon stories.

comment NOUN a remark.

did you know?

comma

- The punctuation mark (,) is called a *comma.*
- Commas are used:
  1 to separate words in a series. *A long, narrow, twisting road.*
  2 to separate longer groups of words. *They walked home, taking a short cut across the fields.*
  3 in a book to separate the words of a spoken sentence from a verb. *He asked, 'Do you want some more ice-cream?'*
  4 to divide large numbers into groups of three digits. *76,813. 1,000,000.*

compass NOUN (PLURAL compasses) an instrument used for showing direction that has a magnetic needle which always points to north.

compass

competition NOUN a contest to find a winner.

computer NOUN an electronic machine that stores and processes information when programmed.

concert NOUN a musical performance. *A rock concert.*

did you know?

conjunction

- A *conjunction* is a word that joins parts of a sentence.
- A conjunction may join two or more words.

  For example, '*and*' is a conjunction in '*fish and chips*'.
- A conjunction may also join groups of words.

  For example, 'because' is a conjunction in '*Don't wear these clothes, because they are still damp.*'

consonant

- A *consonant* is the sound made by any of the letters *b*, *c*, *d*, *f*, *g*, *h*, *j*, *k*, *l*, *m*, *n*, *p*, *q*, *r*, *s*, *t*, *v*, *w*, *x*, *y* and *z*.

conditioner NOUN **1** a liquid that you put on your hair after you have washed it to make it softer. **2** a liquid that you put in your washing machine to make your clothes softer.

container NOUN something that holds something else inside it.

container

continue VERB (continuing, continued) to carry on.

control NOUN **1** power or authority. **2** a switch on a machine.

control VERB (controlling, controlled) to have the power to make people or things behave exactly as you want them to.

cook NOUN a person who prepares and cooks food.

cook VERB to heat food in some way so it can be eaten.

cooker NOUN something that cooks food, an oven.

cool ADJECTIVE **1** not warm and not cold. **2** calm.

copy NOUN (PLURAL copies) **1** something that is made or done like something else. **2** one example of a book or magazine.

copy VERB (copying, copied) to make or do something exactly the same as something else.

cord NOUN thick string.

corn NOUN a crop such as wheat, barley or maize.

corner NOUN **1** the place where two lines, edges or roads meet. **2** a kick from the corner of the field in football.

correct ADJECTIVE right.

correct VERB to make something right, to mark mistakes in something.

cost NOUN the price of something.

costume NOUN **1** a typical style of clothing worn in the past. **2** clothes worn when acting.

costume

cot NOUN a small bed with sides for a baby or young child.

cottage NOUN a small house in the country.

did you know?

costume

During the Victorian period, costumes were very distinctive. People wore different clothes at different times of the day. All women and girls wore corsets and steel or whalebone frames under their dresses. Corsets were worn in order to make their waists look small. They were often very tight and made women faint because they could not breathe properly.

did you know?

cotton

The word *cotton* originally comes from Arabic. Other words from Arabic that have become part of the English language include: *algebra, alcohol, alcove, assassin, carafe, cipher, harem, magazine, mattress, monsoon, sash, sofa, syrup, tariff, zero.*

cotton NOUN **1** a plant which produces soft, white fibre. **2** thread made from the cotton plant. **3** cloth woven from cotton thread.

cotton

cough VERB to push the air noisily from your throat, often because you are ill.

could *See* **can**. *Could I come in?*

couldn't = could not. *We couldn't go to sleep.*

count VERB **1** to say the numbers one after another. **2** to add up.

country NOUN (PLURAL countries) **1** a land with its own government, people, language, etc. **2** the land outside towns and cities.

cousin NOUN the child of your aunt or uncle.

cover NOUN something put over something else to hide or protect it.

cover VERB to put something over something else to hide or protect it.

cow NOUN the female of cattle, kept on farms for milk.

cowboy NOUN a man who herds cattle in America.

crack NOUN **1** a thin line where something has split but not broken completely. **2** a sudden, sharp noise.

crack VERB to split, but not break completely.

crane NOUN a machine for moving heavy things by lifting them into the air.

crash NOUN (PLURAL crashes) **1** an accident involving vehicles. **2** the noise made by things smashing into one another.

crash VERB to hit another vehicle in an accident.

crack

crawl VERB to move forward on your hands and knees like a baby does before it walks.

crayon NOUN a coloured wax stick or pencil for drawing.

crayon

cream NOUN **1** the thick part at the top of the milk. **2** a pale yellow colour. **3** something you rub into your skin.

creep VERB (crept) to move slowly and quietly.

did you know?

cowboy

Although there are still many people in the American West who ride horses and herd cattle, the great days of the cowboys only lasted 40 years, from the 1860s to the 1900s.

There were open grasslands during that time, that stretched from Texas to Canada, where cattle were grazed. They were then driven in great herds by cowboys to railroad stations.

crept *See* **creep**. *We crept along the corridor.*

cricket NOUN **1** a team game played with bats, a ball and wickets. **2** an insect.

crocodile NOUN a large reptile that lives in water and on land.

crooked ADJECTIVE not straight. *A crooked path.*

cross ADJECTIVE bad-tempered.

cross NOUN (PLURAL crosses) two lines that go over each other in the shape of + or ×.

cross VERB **1** to go over from one side to another. *Cross the road.* **2** to make a cross shape. *Cross your legs.*

cry VERB (crying, cried) **1** to let tears fall from your eyes, to weep. **2** to shout out loud.

cub NOUN the young of a wild animal such as a fox, a lion or a wolf.

cuckoo NOUN a bird that lays its eggs in the nests of other birds.

cucumber NOUN a long, thin, round salad vegetable with a green skin.

cuddle VERB (cuddling, cuddled) to show that you love someone by holding them closely in your arms.

cultured ADJECTIVE well educated, with good manners and a knowledge of the arts.

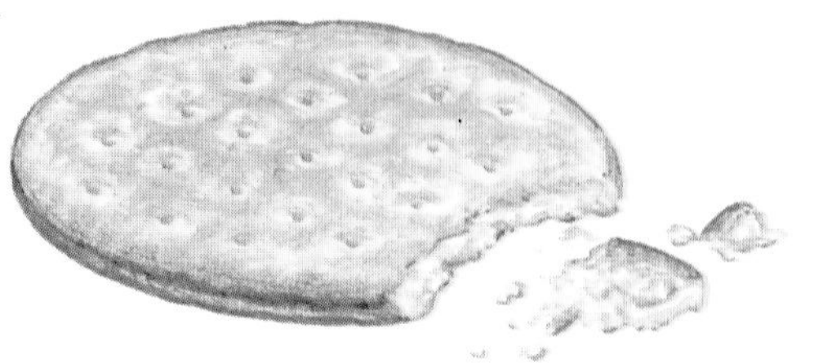

crumb

cupboard NOUN a piece of furniture to put things in.

curb VERB to keep something under control. *The government has curbed the powers of the police.*

curl NOUN a piece of hair curved at the end.

curl VERB to twist into a curved shape.

crocodile

crow NOUN a big, black bird with a loud cry.

crowd NOUN **1** a large gathering of people in a space. **2** the audience at a sporting event or a rock concert.

crown NOUN a circular band, often made of gold and jewels, and worn on the heads of kings and queens.

cruel ADJECTIVE very unkind, deliberately causing pain to others.

crumb NOUN a tiny bit of bread, cake or biscuit.

cup NOUN **1** a small, round container with a handle, from which you drink liquids. **2** a prize given to the winner of a competition.

cup

curler NOUN a pin or roller put in hair to make it curly.

curly ADJECTIVE full of curls. *Curly hair.*

currant NOUN 1 a small dried grape used in baking and cooking. 2 a soft, red, black or white berry. *Redcurrant. Blackcurrant. Whitecurrant.*

current NOUN water, air or electricity that moves in a certain direction. *The ocean currents.*

curry NOUN (PLURAL curries) a hot, spicy meal. *John's favourite food is curry.*

curtain NOUN a piece of material hung over a window to keep out light.

curve NOUN a smooth, bending line.

curve VERB (curving, curved) to bend. *The road curves at the top of the hill.*

curve

cushion NOUN a bag filled with soft material to make you more comfortable when you are sitting on something.

customer NOUN a person who buys something.

cut VERB (cutting) to remove a piece of or make an opening in something.

cute ADJECTIVE pretty, attractive. *She's a cute little girl.*

cycle NOUN a bicycle.

cycling VERB riding on a bicycle.

cycling

cymbals PLURAL NOUN a musical instrument made of two round brass plates that are banged together to make a loud, ringing noise.

cymbals

did you know?

currant

You should not confuse the word *currant*, meaning a small dried grape or a soft berry (*blackcurrant jam*) with the word *current*.

When used as a noun, *current* means 'flow' (*currents of water*; *electric current*).

When used as an adjective, *current* means 'happening at the present time' (*current affairs*).

The words are *homophones* – words that are pronounced the same way but have a different meaning, origin or spelling.

Other examples of homophones are: *bare – bear, rain – reign, right – write, sloe – slow, son – sun, tail – tale, threw – through, too – two, wait – weight.*

Dd

danger

dad, daddy NOUN (PLURAL dads, daddies) a name that children call their father.

daffodil NOUN a yellow flower that grows from a bulb in spring.

daisy NOUN (PLURAL daisies) a wild flower with a yellow centre and white petals.

daisy

damage NOUN harm or injury that is done to something.

damage VERB (damaging, damaged) to harm, injure or spoil something.

damp ADJECTIVE slightly wet, not completely dry.

dance NOUN a series of steps and movements that you make to music.

dance VERB (dancing, danced) to move in time to music.

dandelion NOUN a wild plant with a yellow flower.

danger NOUN something that could bring death or harm.

dangerous ADJECTIVE not safe.

dark ADJECTIVE **1** without much light. *A dark night.* **2** almost black. *Dark hair.*

date NOUN **1** a particular day of the year or the year in which something happened. **2** someone of the opposite sex you arrange to go out with.

daughter NOUN someone's female child.

day NOUN **1** the time from sunrise to sunset. **2** 24 hours.

dead ADJECTIVE not alive.

deaf ADJECTIVE not able to hear.

dear ADJECTIVE **1** much loved. **2** a word that is used to begin a letter. **3** not cheap.

December NOUN the twelfth month of the year.

December

decide VERB (deciding, decided) to make up your mind about something.

decimal ADJECTIVE counting in tens or tenths.

decorate VERB (decorating, decorated) to add things to make something look better or nicer.

decoration NOUN something you add to something else to make it look nicer.

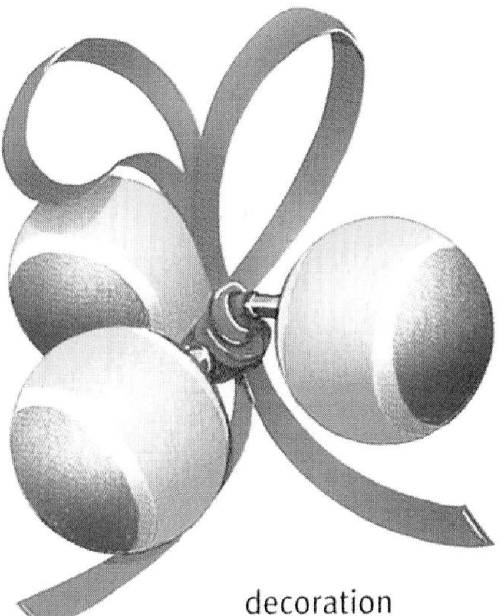
decoration

deep ADJECTIVE **1** going down or back a long way. **2** the measurement of something from top to bottom or from front to back.

deer NOUN (PLURAL deer) a large wild animal, the male of which usually has branched horns (antlers) on its head.

delicious ADJECTIVE good to eat or smell.

delight NOUN great happiness.

delighted ADJECTIVE very pleased and excited.

deliver VERB **1** to send or take something somewhere. **2** to help at the birth of a baby.

dentist NOUN someone who looks after your teeth.

depth NOUN the measurement of something such as a river between the surface and the bottom.

describe VERB (describing, described) to say what something or someone is like.

desert NOUN a large area of sandy land that does not get a lot of rain and in which very few plants grow.

design VERB to plan or draw something to show how you can make it.

desk NOUN a piece of furniture that you sit at to read or write.

desert

did you know?

dialect

A dialect is the form of a language that is spoken in a particular area.

destroy VERB to ruin something so that it can't be mended.

dew NOUN very small drops of water that form on the ground overnight.

diagram

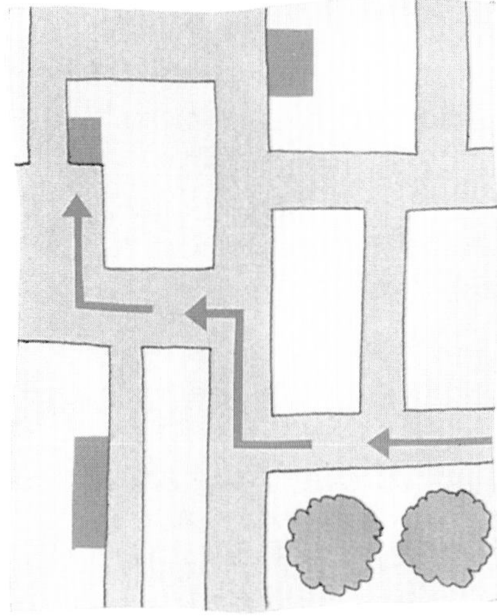

diagram NOUN a drawing that shows or explains something.

diamond NOUN **1** a precious jewel. **2** a shape with four equal sides that stands on one of its points.

diary NOUN (PLURAL diaries) a book marked off with the days of the year so that you can write in it the things you have planned to do or have done.

dice NOUN (PLURAL dice) a small cube with spots from one to six on each of its sides, used in playing some games.

dice

did *See* **do**. *Yesterday I did not have any homework to do.*

didn't = did not. *Yesterday I didn't have any homework.*

die VERB (dying, died) to stop living.

diesel NOUN **1** a vehicle with an oil-burning engine. **2** the kind of fuel used in a diesel engine.

did you know?

dictionary

A dictionary is a book that gives you a list of the words of a language and their meaning.

dig

different ADJECTIVE not like another person or thing.

difficult ADJECTIVE hard to do or understand.

dig VERB (dug) to move earth to break it up or to make a hole.

dinner NOUN the main meal of the day that is eaten either in the middle of the day or in the evening.

dinosaur

dinosaur NOUN a large prehistoric animal that is now extinct.

dip NOUN **1** something that is lower. *A dip in the road.* **2** a quick swim. **3** a mixture that you dip other foods into.

dip VERB (dipping, dipped) **1** to put something into a liquid and to take it out again quickly. **2** to make something lower. *Dip your headlights.*

direction NOUN the way in which someone or something is moving, pointing or is aimed at.

dirt NOUN mud, dust or anything that is not clean.

dirty

dirty ADJECTIVE (dirtier, dirtiest) not clean.

disabled ADJECTIVE not able to use a part of your body properly.

disappear VERB to go out of sight.

disappoint VERB to be sad because something you expected or hoped for didn't happen. *We were disappointed that it rained.*

disaster NOUN an unexpected event that causes a lot of damage or suffering.

disco NOUN a place where you can dance to pop music.

discover VERB to find out something, especially for the first time. *I discovered a short-cut to the shops.*

disguise NOUN something you wear so that people will not recognize you.

disguise VERB (disguising, disguised) to change the appearance of something so people will not recognize it.

dish NOUN (PLURAL dishes) a bowl or plate that food is served from.

dishwasher NOUN a machine that cleans the dirty plates, pots and pans that you use when cooking and eating a meal.

disk NOUN a flat piece of plastic with magnetic material that stores information used in a computer.

distance NOUN how far it is between two places.

disturb VERB to interrupt what someone is doing or someone's rest. *Don't disturb him; he's asleep.*

dive VERB (diving, dived) to jump into water head first.

dive

doll

divide VERB (dividing, divided) **1** to share out or separate into smaller parts. **2** to find out how many times one number will go into another. *Ten divided by two is five.*

dizzy ADJECTIVE (dizzier, dizziest) feeling as if you are going to fall over.

do VERB (does, doing, did, done) **1** to perform an action. *Do the dishes.* **2** to be suitable. *That'll do.* **3** used in questions. *Do you like it?* **4** used to form negatives. *Don't throw the ball here.* **5** to cause. *Smoking can do you a lot of harm.* **6** to work at. *'What does she do for a living?' 'She's a banker.'*

doctor NOUN someone who looks after you when you are ill.

does *See* **do**. *Does your grandma live with you?*

doesn't = does not. *Our grandma doesn't live with us.*

dog NOUN a four-legged animal that barks, usually kept as a pet.

doll NOUN a toy that looks like a person.

dolphin NOUN a large wild animal that lives in the sea.

done *See* **do**. *I haven't done anything to my model railway for a few days.*

don't = do not. *Don't touch the radiator – it's very hot.*

donkey NOUN an animal that looks like a horse, but is smaller and has longer ears.

donkey

door NOUN something on hinges or runners that opens and closes to let you in or out of a building, room or vehicle.

dot NOUN a small, round spot.

double VERB (doubling, doubled) to make two of something, to make twice as much.

down 1 in a direction from a higher to a lower place. **2** along. *Down the road.*

downstairs the ground floor.

did you know?

dog

A dog is our familiar household pet. The word *dog* is also used to mean the male of this kind of animal (the female is a bitch). The word *dog* is also used for the male of other animals, such as the fox (female, vixen) and the wolf (female, bitch).

dozen NOUN twelve of anything.

drag VERB (dragging, dragged) to pull something heavy along.

drain VERB to let water run out of something.

drank *See* **drink**. *I drank juice with my lunch.*

draw VERB (drew, drawn) **1** to make a picture. **2** to end a game or a contest without either side winning.

drawer NOUN something you put things in that slides in and out of a piece of furniture.

drawing NOUN a picture made with crayons, pencils, etc.

draw

drawn *See* **draw**. *Our team has drawn six matches this season.*

dream NOUN **1** something you seem to see when you sleep. **2** something you think about that you'd like to happen.

dream VERB (dreamt or dreamed) to seem to see when you are sleeping.

dream

dreamt or **dreamed** *See* **dream**. *I dreamt I was travelling on a flying carpet.*

dress NOUN (PLURAL dresses) a piece of female clothing with a top and a skirt all in one.

dressing gown NOUN what you wear over your night clothes when you are not quite ready to get into bed.

drew *See* **draw**. *Yesterday we drew pictures of birds.*

drill NOUN a tool for making holes in things.

drill VERB to make a hole in something.

drink NOUN a liquid you can drink, especially alcohol.

drink VERB (drank, drunk) **1** to swallow any kind of liquid. **2** to swallow a lot of alcohol.

drip VERB (dripping, dripped) to fall in drops.

drive VERB (driving, drove, driven) to be able to control a vehicle.

driven *See* **drive**. *Have you ever driven a car in another country?*

drizzle NOUN fine rain.

drop NOUN **1** a small amount of liquid. **2** a sweet. *Pear drops.* **3** a fall. *A drop of 100 metres.*

drop VERB (dropping, dropped) to fall straight down.

drove *See* **drive**. *We drove to Birmingham to the Motor Show.*

drown VERB to die because of not being able to breathe underwater.

drum NOUN **1** a musical instrument that you bang with a stick. **2** a large container. *An oil drum.*

drums PLURAL NOUN lots of different sized drums played by a drummer in a band or orchestra.

drunk *See* **drink**. *I've drunk too much cola.*

dry ADJECTIVE (drier, driest) not wet.

duck NOUN a water bird with webbed feet.

dug *See* **dig**. *We dug the garden at the weekend.*

dump VERB to get rid of something that you do not want.

during throughout all the time.

drip

dust NOUN small bits of dirt.

dust VERB **1** to clean dust off something. **2** to sprinkle with powder.

dustbin NOUN a big container that you put your rubbish in outside your house.

duvet NOUN a large material-filled cover for a bed instead of sheets and blankets.

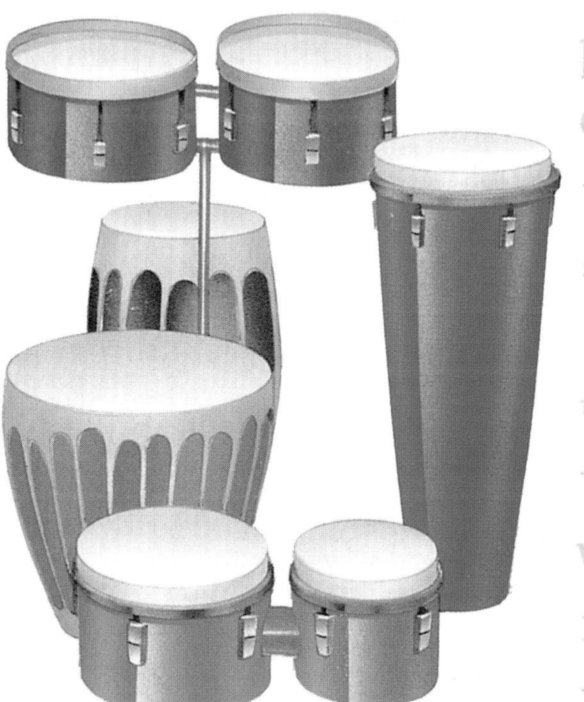
drum

eagle

Ee

each every one.

eagle NOUN a large bird of prey.

ear NOUN one of the two openings on the side of your head with which you hear.

early ADJECTIVE (earlier, earliest) **1** near the start of the day. **2** before the normal or right time.

earn VERB to receive money for work that you do.

earth NOUN **1** the planet that we live on. **2** soil, the ground.

earthquake NOUN a sudden and violent movement of the ground, often causing much damage.

east

east NOUN one of the four points of the compass, the direction of the rising sun.

Easter NOUN the time of year when Christians celebrate the death of Jesus and his coming back to life again.

did you know?

Earth

Earth is thought to be between 4 and 5 billion years old and as far as we know, the only planet that supports life. Until about 500 years ago it was thought that the Earth was flat. People believed that if a ship sailed too far east or west, it would fall over the edge of the Earth. The early voyages of discovery proved what we know today, that the Earth is round.

easy ADJECTIVE (easier, easiest) not difficult to do.

eat VERB (ate, eaten) to put food in your mouth and swallow it.

Easter

eaten *See* **eat**. *We've eaten all the cakes.*

echo NOUN (PLURAL echoes) a sound that bounces off a surface and is heard again.

edge NOUN **1** the sharp, cutting part of a knife, tool, etc. **2** the place or line that marks the beginning or end of something.

eel NOUN a long fish that looks like a snake.

egg NOUN **1** the round shell-covered object laid by birds and some other creatures and from which their babies come. **2** a hen's egg, eaten as food.

egg

eight the number 8.

eighteen the number 18.

eighty the number 80.

8

eight

did you know?

electricity

The earliest form of electricity was static electricity. A slight shock was produced by rubbing a piece of amber.

The Greek for amber is *elektron* and so the word *electricity*, coined in the 17th century, came into being.

either one or the other of two people or things.

elbow NOUN the part of your arm where it bends.

electric ADJECTIVE worked by electricity.

electricity NOUN the energy that travels along power lines that we use for lighting, heating and making machines work.

elephant NOUN a very big animal with tusks and a trunk.

eleven the number 11.

elephant

emerald NOUN a precious, green jewel.

emerald

empty ADJECTIVE (emptier, emptiest) with nothing inside. *An empty glass.*

end NOUN **1** the point where something stops or finishes. **2** the time when something stops.

end VERB to stop or finish.

enemy NOUN (PLURAL enemies) someone who is against you and wants to harm you.

energy NOUN **1** physical strength to do something. **2** power from electricity, coal, etc., to drive machinery.

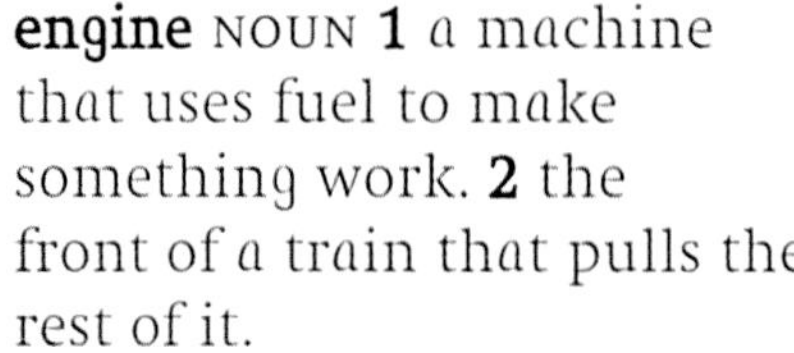

engine NOUN **1** a machine that uses fuel to make something work. **2** the front of a train that pulls the rest of it.

enjoy VERB to take pleasure in something.

enormous ADJECTIVE very big.

enough as much or as many as you need.

enter VERB to go into a place.

entrance

enthusiastic ADJECTIVE showing great excitement or approval about something.

entrance NOUN the way in. *The front entrance.*

envelope NOUN a paper cover inside which you put a letter or card.

equal ADJECTIVE the same in number, size, value, etc. *All the portions are equal.*

escalator NOUN a moving staircase.

escape VERB (escaping, escaped) to get away or to break free.

evergreen

especially 1 more than usual. **2** more special.

estate car NOUN a car with a door at the back and extra space behind the back seats.

even still, yet, more than expected. *Today was even hotter than yesterday.*

even ADJECTIVE **1** smooth and flat. **2** equal. **3** that can be divided exactly by two. *2, 4 and 6 are even numbers.*

evening NOUN the time at the end of the day and the beginning of the night.

eventually at the end of a lot of delays, finally.

ever 1 at any time. *No one ever comes to see us.* **2** at all times. *For ever and ever.* **3** said to emphasize something. *I'm ever so tired.*

evergreen NOUN a tree or bush that has green leaves through all the year.

every all, each one.

everybody everyone, every person. *Everybody is welcome.*

everything all, each thing together. *Everything must go.*

evil ADJECTIVE very bad or wicked.

evil NOUN a force that causes very bad things to happen.

excellent ADJECTIVE very good indeed. *He is an excellent tennis player.*

did you know?

ex

The prefix ex- is used to mean:

1 out of: exit, expel, explode;

2 former: ex-husband, ex-wife, ex-president.

except apart from. *The film's alright, except that it's too long.*

excited ADJECTIVE very happy and enthusiastic, especially because you are looking forward to something.

excuse NOUN a reason that you give to explain why you have done something or not done something.

excuse VERB (excusing, excused) to say why you did something.

exercise NOUN **1** movements that you do to keep fit. **2** something that you do to train or practise for something.

excercise

did you know?

exclamation mark

- The sign (!) is called an *exclamation mark*.
- It is used with words that express strong feelings such as shock, surprise or urgency.

'Oh bother!' 'Ouch!'
'What fun we had that day!' cried the twins.
'Hurry up, boys! You'll miss the bus,' Mum called out.

'Hooray! I'm sure we've won,' James called to his friends on the football field.

explode

exercise VERB (exercising, exercised) to do sports, walk, etc., in order to become fit and healthy.

exhibition NOUN a collection of things for people to go to see.

exit NOUN the way out.

exhibition

expect VERB **1** to suppose that something is going to happen. **2** to wait for.

expensive ADJECTIVE costing a lot of money.

explain VERB to give the meaning of something so that someone else can understand. *I explained how the tourists could get to the museum.*

explode VERB (exploding, exploded) to blow up with a loud bang.

explore VERB (exploring, explored) to go somewhere that you have not been to before to discover what it is like. *We explored the dangerous jungle with excitement.*

explosion NOUN a loud bang made when something explodes. *The noise of the explosion was very loud.*

extra ADJECTIVE another or more besides. *The vitamin tablets give her extra strength.*

extremely very.

eye NOUN one of the two parts of your face with which you see.

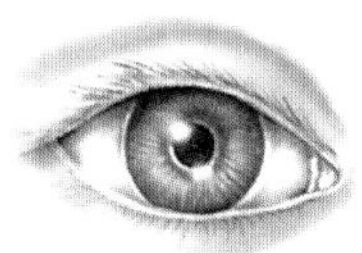
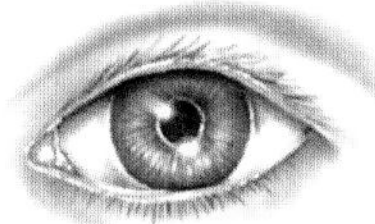

eyes

did you know?

eye

A small lizard-like animal found only in New Zealand, called the sphenodon or tuatara has a primitive third eye. Its purpose is unknown. The biggest species of whale have eyes about 10cm across.

A B C D E F G H I J K L M N O P Q R S T U V W X Y Z

Ff

face NOUN **1** the front of your head from your hair to your chin. **2** the front of anything. *A clock face.*

face

face VERB (facing, faced) **1** to be opposite. *Facing the station.* **2** to deal with. *Face a problem.*

fact NOUN a piece of information that is true. *That's a fact.*

factory NOUN (PLURAL factories) a place where things are made by machines. *A car factory.*

fair ADJECTIVE **1** honest, sticking to the rules. *A fair contest.* **2** light in colour. *Fair skin.* **3** not bad, average. *A fair number of people.*

fair NOUN a show with rides, games, stalls, etc.

family

fairy NOUN (PLURAL fairies) a tiny, imaginary, winged creature who does magic.

fairy

fairy tale NOUN a children's story about fairies and magic. *The fairy tale had a happy ending.*

fall VERB (fell, fallen) **1** to drop down. *Snow was falling outside.* **2** to get lower. *The ground falls away steeply.*

fallen *See* **fall**. *Part of the roof has fallen down.*

false ADJECTIVE untrue or incorrect. *The information that I read in yesterday's newspaper turned out to be false.*

family NOUN (PLURAL families) **1** parents together with their children. **2** a group of people who are related. **3** any group of things or creatures that are alike or related.

famous ADJECTIVE well known by lots of people.

fan NOUN **1** something that makes air move to keep you cool. **2** an enthusiastic supporter of something.

fan

far a long way off.

farm NOUN buildings and land used for growing crops or keeping animals.

farmer NOUN someone who owns or looks after a farm. *The farmer kept sheep.*

did you know?

favourite

The American spelling of *favourite* is *favorite*. Other examples of the differences between British and American spellings include: British *colour* – American *color*; British *labour* – American *labor*; British *centre* – American *center*; British *fibre* – American *fiber*; British *theatre* – American *theater*.

fast ADJECTIVE **1** quick. **2** firmly fixed. *Stuck fast.* **3** ahead of time. *My watch is ten minutes fast.*

fasten VERB to fix or close.

fat ADJECTIVE (fatter, fattest) **1** having too much flesh on your body, overweight. **2** thick and round.

father

father NOUN a man who has a child.

fault NOUN a mistake in something.

favourite ADJECTIVE that is liked the best.

fax NOUN (PLURAL faxes) **1** information on paper sent electronically down a telephone line. **2** the machine that sends such information.

fax VERB to send information using a fax machine.

feathers

fear NOUN the feeling of being afraid, the feeling that danger is near.

feather NOUN one of the many soft, light coverings on a bird.

February

February NOUN the second month of the year after January and before March.

fed *See* **feed**. *Have you fed the rabbits today?*

feed

feed VERB (fed) to give food to someone. *The mother feeds her children.*

feel VERB (felt) **1** to touch. *Feel the texture.* **2** to experience something. *Feel terrified.* **3** to think. *He feels that eating meat is wrong.*

feet *See* **foot**.

fell *See* **fall**. *He tripped and fell.*

felt *See* **feel**. *After the bumpy ride, I felt ill.*

female NOUN a person or animal that can produce babies or young.

did you know?

female

The names of female animals include: *doe* (deer), *bitch* (dog), *vixen* (fox), *nanny-goat* (goat), *mare* (horse), *lioness* (lion), *sow* (pig), *doe* (rabbit), and *ewe* (sheep).

fence NOUN a barrier made of wood or wire that goes round a field or garden.

fence

fetch VERB to go to get something and bring it back.

fever NOUN an illness which gives you a very high temperature.

few not a lot.

field NOUN **1** an area of land surrounded by a fence or hedge, in which crops are grown or animals are kept. **2** any area where sports are played or something else takes place. *A battlefield.*

fierce ADJECTIVE cruel and angry.

fifteen the number 15.

fifty the number 50.

fight VERB (fought) **1** to try to hurt someone. **2** to struggle to get something.

figure NOUN **1** a number. **2** the shape of someone's body, especially a woman's body.

fill VERB to make something full.

film NOUN **1** a movie shown in the cinema. **2** something you put in your camera so that you can take photographs.

finally coming last, at the end. *Finally over.*

find VERB (found) **1** to discover something you have lost. **2** to learn, to work out.

fine ADJECTIVE **1** very thin. *Fine silk.* **2** (of weather) dry, bright. *A fine day.*

fine NOUN money you have to pay if you do something wrong.

finger NOUN one of the four parts of your body at the end of each hand.

finish VERB to stop, to end.

fine

fire NOUN **1** something that burns and gives out heat and light. **2** a gas or electric heater.

fire engine NOUN a large vehicle used to put out fires.

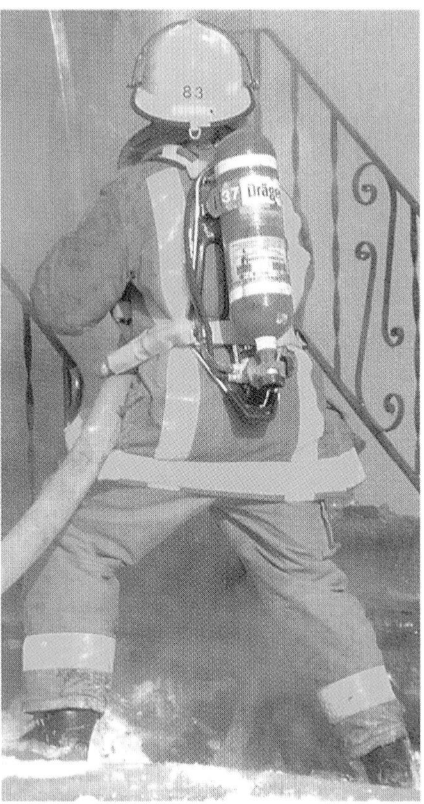

firefighter

firefighter NOUN someone whose job is to put out fires.

fireworks PLURAL NOUN small chemical devices that burn and make noises to entertain people.

did you know?

firefighter

These days we use the same word to describe both men and women who do a particular job. This is in place of different words for men and women.

Other examples are: *camera operator* (rather than *cameraman*, *camerawoman*), *firefighter* (rather than *fireman*, *firewoman*), *headteacher* (rather than *headmaster*, *headmistress*), *police officer* (rather than *policeman*, *policewoman*).

first ADJECTIVE **1** before any others. **2** the most important.

5

five

fish NOUN (PLURAL fishes) a creature that swims and lives in water and breathes through gills.

fishing NOUN the industry or sport of catching fish.

fist NOUN a tightly closed hand. *Clenched fist.*

fishes

fit ADJECTIVE (fitter, fittest) healthy. *The runner became very fit after training for the New York marathon.*

fit VERB (fitting, fitted) to be the right size and shape.

five the number 5.

fix VERB **1** to fasten something firmly. **2** to decide on something. *We've fixed a date for the wedding.* **3** to mend something.

flood

flag NOUN a piece of cloth used as a sign or signal.

flame NOUN a red or yellow tongue of fire.

flash VERB to shine suddenly and briefly.

flat ADJECTIVE (flatter, flattest) **1** smooth and level. **2** below the right musical note. **3** without any air. *A flat tyre.*

flat NOUN home with the rooms on one floor of a larger building.

flavour NOUN the taste of something.

flew *See* **fly**. *The birds flew away.*

float VERB to stay on the top of a liquid without sinking, or to be kept up in the air. *My toy boat floated on the pond.*

flood NOUN water that covers what is usually dry land.

foor NOUN **1** the part of a building or room that you stand on. **2** all the rooms on the same level in a building.

flour NOUN a fine, white powder made from grain and used for baking.

flow VERB to run smoothly. *The wine flowed from the bottle.*

flower NOUN the part of a plant with petals and containing the seeds.

flown *See* **fly**. *Have you ever flown in an aeroplane?*

flu NOUN an illness like a very bad cold that gives you a temperature and makes you ache.

a b c d e f g h i j k l m n o p q r s t u v w x y z

A B C D E F G H I J K L M N O P Q R S T U V W X Y Z

flute NOUN a musical instrument that you blow into.

fly NOUN (PLURAL flies) a flying insect.

fly VERB (flew, flown) **1** to move through the air like a bird. **2** to go in an aeroplane.

fog NOUN thick mist.

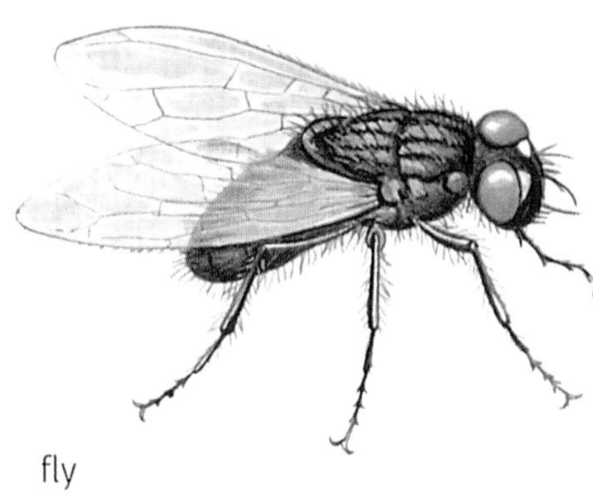

fly

fold VERB to bend something over on itself.

fog

follow VERB **1** to go after someone or something. **2** to support. *They follow their local football team.* **3** to understand. *Do you follow my meaning?*

food NOUN something you can eat.

foot NOUN (PLURAL feet) **1** the part of your body that you stand on. **2** a measurement equal to 12 inches or 0.305 metres.

football NOUN a team game in which you kick a ball and try to score goals.

footpath NOUN a path for you to walk on, especially in the countryside.

for 1 to be given to, to be meant for. *This present is for you.* **2** instead of. *New for old.* **3** as long as, as far as. *I ran for two miles.* **4** because of. *We couldn't see you for the crowds.* **5** at a cost of. *You can buy that for £1.*

did you know?

forest

There are a number of different types of forest. Tropical rainforests are found near the equator. Many kinds of plants and trees grow very quickly in this hot climate.

Deciduous forests, with trees such as oak and beech, are found in temperate lands such as Europe and cooler parts of Africa. Coniferous forests, nearly always found in northern lands, are mostly made up of one type of tree such as spruce, pine or fir.

forehead NOUN the part of your face below your hair and above your eyebrows.

forehead

forest NOUN a large area of land thickly covered with trees.

forgave *See* **forgive**. *He said sorry so she forgave him.*

forget VERB (forgot, forgotten) not to remember. *Try not to forget your coat.*

forgive VERB (forgiving, forgave, forgiven) to stop wanting to punish someone who has done something wrong.

forgiven *See* **forgive**. *I've forgiven you for what you did.*

forgot, forgotten *See* **forget**. *They forgot to come to tea. I've forgotten my computer password.*

fork NOUN **1** something with a handle and prongs that you use to eat your food with. *Eat with a knife and fork.* **2** a tool with a handle and prongs for digging the earth. *The fork is kept in the shed.*

did you know?

Friday

Friday is named after the Scandinavian goddess *Frigg*, the goddess of love. This was an alteration to the Latin *Veneris dies*, the day of Venus, the Roman goddess of love.

fortunate ADJECTIVE lucky.

fortune NOUN **1** good luck. **2** fate, what will happen in the future. *The old woman told him his fortune.*

forty the number 40.

forwards towards the front. *We moved forwards to the front of the crowd.*

fossil NOUN the remains of an animal or plant that have hardened and left a print in rock.

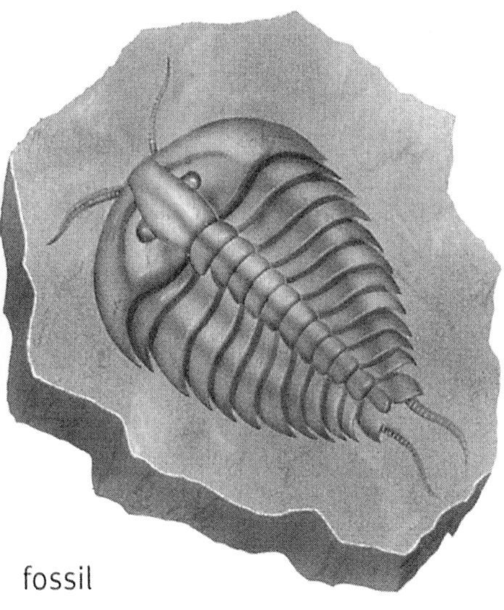

fossil

foster child NOUN a boy or girl who is officially looked after by parents who are not the natural parents.

fought *See* **fight**. *The soldiers fought in the war.*

found *See* **find**. *We found the keys down the side of the sofa.*

four the number 4.

four

fourteen the number 14.

fox NOUN (PLURAL foxes) a wild animal like a dog, but with a bushy tail.

fox

frame NOUN the structure surrounding a window, door, picture, etc.

free ADJECTIVE **1** able to do whatever you like. **2** not costing anything. **3** not being used.

freeze VERB (freezing, froze, frozen) to turn something hard and solid by making it very cold.

freezer NOUN a place to keep frozen food.

fresh ADJECTIVE **1** just made. *Fresh bread.* **2** just picked or grown. *Fresh vegetables.* **3** clean and pure. *Fresh air.*

fresh vegetables

Friday NOUN the day of the week after Thursday and before Saturday. *I'll see you on Friday.*

friend NOUN someone you know well and like to spend time with. *She has a lot of good friends.*

friendly ADJECTIVE (friendlier, friendliest) behaving in a kind and helpful way. *He is very friendly.*

frighten VERB to make someone afraid. *The dog frightened me when it barked.*

frill NOUN **1** strip of pleated paper or cloth attached to something as a decoration. *A frill on a dress.* **2** an unnecessary extra, a luxury. *No frills.*

frilly ADJECTIVE *He bought a frilly lampshade.*

A B C D E **F** G H I J K L M N O P Q R S T U V W X Y Z

frog NOUN a small animal that lives on land and in water and has long legs for jumping.

frog

from used to show where something begins. *Smoke comes from a fire.*

front NOUN **1** the position facing forwards. **2** the most important position.

frontier NOUN the border where one country meets another. *Eastern frontier.*

frost NOUN white, powdery ice that forms outdoors in freezing weather.

frown VERB to wrinkle your forehead when you are cross or worried.

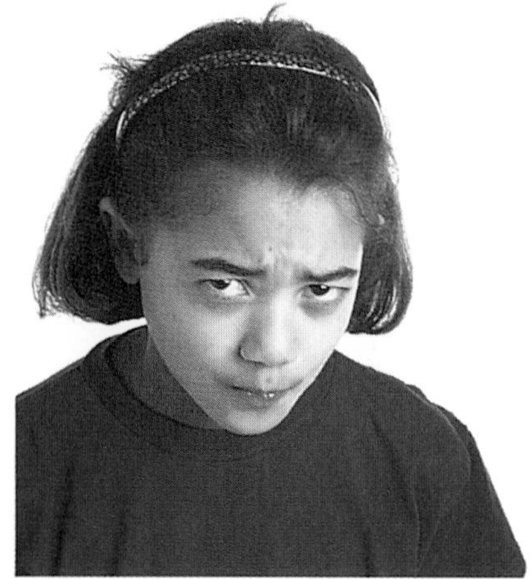

frown

froze, frozen *See* **freeze**. *The water froze to form ice. The lake has frozen over.*

fruit NOUN the part of a plant that has the seeds in it and can often be eaten.

fry VERB (frying, fried) to cook in hot oil or fat.

full ADJECTIVE holding as much as is possible.

full

full stop The punctuation mark (.) is called a *full stop*. It is used: **1** at the end of a sentence. *Jo came to our house.* **2** after short forms of a word (abbreviations) and initial letters that stand for a whole word: *'Jan.'* stands for *'January'*.

fun NOUN enjoyment. *We had lots of fun at the fair.*

funny ADJECTIVE (funnier, funniest) **1** something that makes you laugh. **2** odd, strange. *My friend tells funny jokes that make me laugh.*

fur NOUN the soft hair on some animals.

furniture PLURAL NOUN things that you need in a room like chairs, cupboards, tables, etc.

furry ADJECTIVE (furrier, furriest) covered in thick, soft hair. *They had lots of furry kittens in the pet shop.*

future NOUN the period of time after the present.

furry

did you know?

fruit

How many different kinds of fruit do you know?

Apple, apricot, avocado, banana, bilberry, blackberry, blackcurrant, cherry, clementine, crab apple, cranberry, damson, fig, gooseberry, grape, grapefruit, greengage, kiwi fruit, lemon, lime, loganberry, lychee, mandarin, mango, melon, nectarine, orange, peach, pear, pineapple, plum, raspberry, redcurrant, rhubarb, satsuma, strawberry, tangerine, ugli fruit, watermelon.

Fruit is an important part of a healthy diet. Fruits contain vitamins and are a good source of fibre, which helps digestion.

Gg

geese

gale NOUN a very strong wind.

gallop NOUN the fastest speed at which a horse can move.

gallop VERB to move at this speed, to move very fast.

game NOUN something you play, usually with rules.

gap NOUN a narrow opening or space.

garage NOUN **1** a place to keep your car. **2** a place where you can take your car to be mended or to get fuel.

garden NOUN land, often by a house, where plants are grown.

gas NOUN **1** something like air that is neither solid nor liquid. **2** fuel used for cooking and heating.

gate NOUN a barrier like a door which opens to let you go through a fence, wall, hedge, etc.

gave *See* **give**. *We gave Ben his birthday present.*

game

geese *See* **goose**.

gel NOUN a smooth, soft substance like jelly which you put on your hair to keep it in a particular style.

gentle ADJECTIVE kind, calm and quiet.

geography NOUN the study of the earth and how people live.

gerbil NOUN a small animal like a large mouse that is kept as a pet.

get VERB (getting, got) **1** to have. **2** to buy. **3** to catch an illness.

ghost NOUN a spirit that appears and looks like a dead person.

ghost

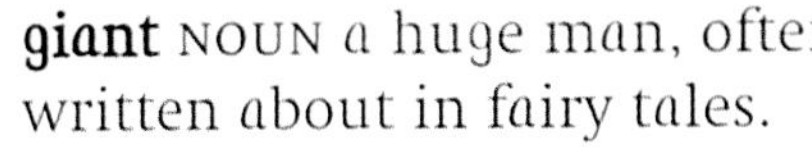

giant NOUN a huge man, often written about in fairy tales.

gift NOUN a present.

giggle VERB (giggling, giggled) to laugh in a nervous or silly way.

giraffe NOUN tall, wild animal with a long neck and legs.

giraffe

girl NOUN a female child.

give VERB (giving, gave, given) **1** to let someone have something to keep. **2** to show or tell. *To give a talk.*

given *See* **give**. *Have you given her the present?*

glad ADJECTIVE (gladder, gladdest) happy and pleased.

A B C D E F **G** H I J K L M N O P Q R S T U V W X Y Z

glass NOUN (PLURAL glasses) **1** hard, clear material used in windows. **2** something made of this that you drink out of.

glasses PLURAL NOUN something you wear over your eyes to help you to see better or to protect them, also called spectacles.

glasses

gloves PLURAL NOUN something you wear on your hands to keep them warm or to protect them.

glue NOUN a substance that sticks things together.

go VERB (went, gone) **1** to start or move. *On your marks, get set, go!* **2** to travel. *Go abroad.* **3** to reach. *Does this road go to the beach?* **4** to work. *Is the clock going?*

goal NOUN **1** the posts between which the ball is aimed in football and some other games. **2** the point scored when the ball passes between the posts. **3** something that you aim for or want to achieve.

goat NOUN a hairy animal with horns that looks a bit like a sheep.

gold NOUN **1** a precious yellow metal. **2** the colour of this metal.

goldfish NOUN a small, often golden, fish usually kept indoors in a tank as a pet.

goldfish

golf NOUN an outdoor game in which a small hard ball is hit with clubs into various holes on a course.

gone *See* **go**. *Sarah has gone on holiday.*

good ADJECTIVE **1** pleasant, satisfactory. *Have a good time.* **2** kind. *They were good to us.* **3** well-behaved. *Good dog!* **4** used in greeting someone. *Good evening.*

goodbye said when you leave someone.

goose NOUN (PLURAL geese) a big bird with webbed feet.

got *See* **get**. *Have you got any books on France?*

grab VERB (grabbing, grabbed) to take hold of something suddenly and roughly.

did you know?

glove

In some other European languages the word for *glove* is related to the word for 'hand'.

For example: German 'Handschuh' and Dutch 'handschoen' mean literally 'hand shoe'.

gram NOUN a measurement of weight equal to 0.01kg.

grandfather NOUN the father of your mother or father.

grandmother NOUN the mother of your mother or father.

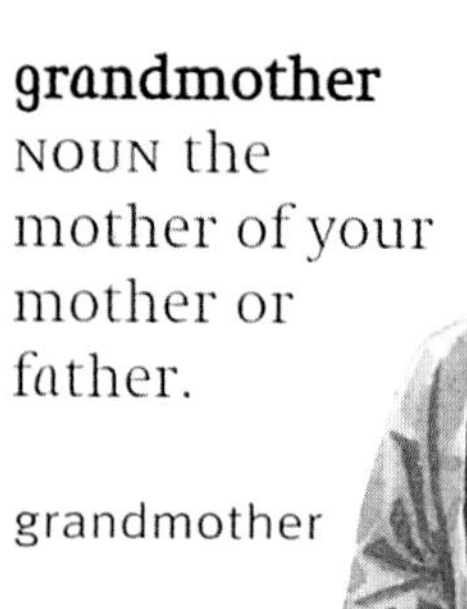
grandmother

grape NOUN a small green or purple fruit that grows in bunches and is used to make wine.

grapes

grapefruit NOUN a round yellow fruit with a slightly bitter taste.

grass NOUN a green plant that is food for cows, sheep, horses, etc.

gravy NOUN a brown sauce that you eat with meat.

great ADJECTIVE **1** very big. **2** very good. **3** unusually clever or important.

green NOUN having the colour of grass.

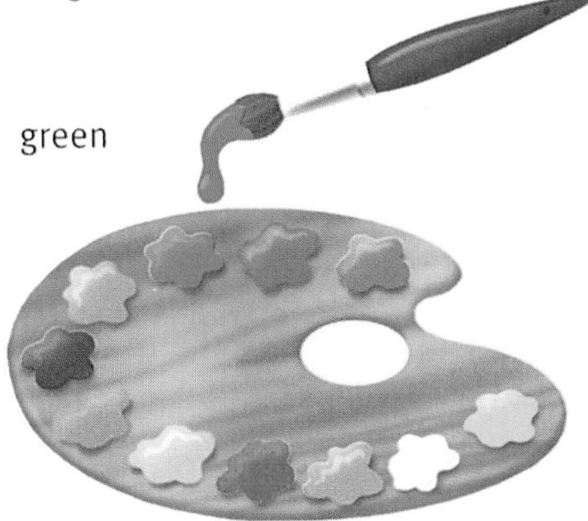
green

greengrocer NOUN someone who sells fruit and vegetables.

grew *See* **grow**. *The tree grew very tall.*

grey ADJECTIVE having the colour of ashes or rain clouds.

grill NOUN a metal implement used to cook food over a strong heat.

grill VERB to cook something under a flame or strong heat.

ground NOUN **1** the surface of the earth. **2** soil. **3** a piece of land where you can play a sport.

group NOUN a number of people or things gathered together.

grow VERB (grew, grown) **1** to get bigger. **2** to live and develop. **3** to plant and water flowers, vegetables, etc. **4** to become. *The nights are growing colder.*

grown *See* **grow**. *I have grown ten centimetres.*

grown-up NOUN a fully grown person, an adult.

guard NOUN **1** someone who watches over something or someone. **2** someone in charge of a train. **3** something that protects you from harm. *A fire-guard.*

guard VERB to protect.

guess VERB to give an answer to something when you are not sure whether it is right or wrong, to estimate. *I guessed the answer to the sum, but I'm not sure that it was right.*

guinea pig NOUN a small, furry animal that can be kept as a pet.

grill

guard

guitar NOUN a stringed musical instrument played with the fingers. *I am learning to play the guitar.*

guinea pig

gun NOUN a weapon that fires bullets.

gym NOUN a place where you can go to train and exercise your body.

A B C D E F G H I J K L M N O P Q R S T U V W X Y Z

Hh

hammer

habit NOUN something that you do often or regularly.

had *See* **have**. I had finished.

hadn't = had not. *If they hadn't told us, we wouldn't have heard the news.*

hail NOUN drops of frozen rain.

hair NOUN **1** fine threads that grow on your skin, especially on your head, and also on the skin of animals. **2** a single one of these.

hairdresser NOUN someone who washes, cuts and styles hair.

half NOUN (PLURAL halves) one of the two equal parts that something is divided into, written as 0.5 or $\frac{1}{2}$.

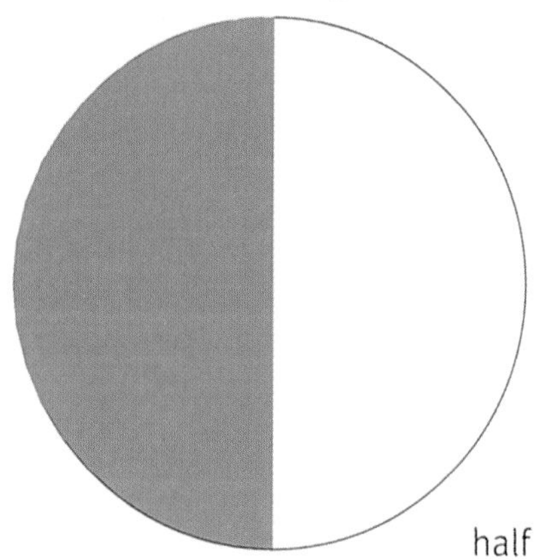
half

half-brother/sister NOUN a brother/sister in your family who has only one of the same parents as you, rather than both.

halves *See* **half**.

hall NOUN **1** the part of a house that is just inside the front door. **2** a big room that can be used for meetings, dances, etc.

ham NOUN meat that comes from a pig's leg.

hamburger NOUN a round cake of chopped beef that you eat fried or grilled in a bun.

hamburger

did you know?

hat

How many different kinds of hat do you know?

Balaclava, baseball cap, bearskin, beret, bobble hat, bonnet, bowler, busby, deerstalker, fez, flat-cap, helmet, homburg, hood, mitre, mortar-board, panama, peaked cap, skullcap, snood, sombrero, sou'wester, stetson, straw hat, sunhat, Tam o'Shanter, top-hat, trilby, turban, yarmulka.

hammer NOUN a tool used for hitting nails, etc., into things.

hamster NOUN a little, furry animal kept indoors in a cage as a pet.

hand NOUN **1** the part of your body at the end of your arm. **2** the part of a clock that points to the time.

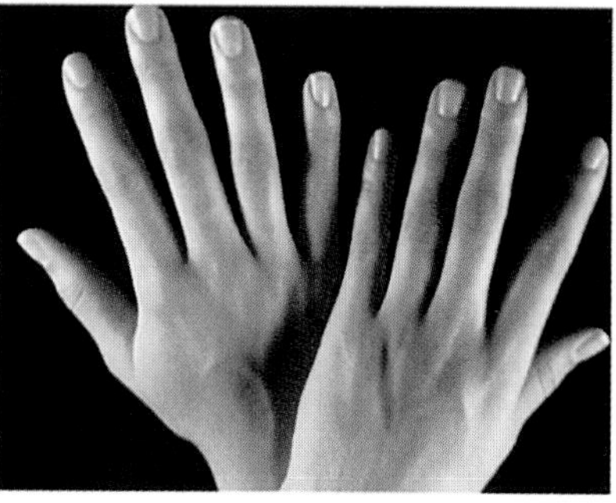
hands

handkerchief NOUN a square piece of material on which you blow your nose.

handle NOUN the part of something you hold it by.

handle VERB (handling, handled) to hold something in your hands.

hang VERB (hung or hanged) **1** to fix something at the top, leaving the lower part free. *I hung the washing on the line and left it to dry.* **2** to kill or die by having a rope tied round your neck.

happen VERB to take place. *Something important is going to happen.*

happy ADJECTIVE pleased or glad.

hard ADJECTIVE **1** solid, not soft. **2** difficult to do.

has *See* **have**. *It has started to rain.*

hasn't = has not. *It hasn't snowed this year.*

hat NOUN something that you wear on your head.

hat

hatch NOUN an opening in a wall, usually for passing food and dishes through from a kitchen to a dining-room.

hatch VERB to break out of an egg, as a baby bird does.

hatchback NOUN a car with a door at the back that opens upwards.

hate VERB (hating, hated) to dislike someone or something very much.

haunted ADJECTIVE a place said to be visited by a ghost.

have VERB (has, having, had) **1** to own. **2** to receive. **3** to enjoy or experience. **4** to get something done. *I have to do my homework.*

heart

haven't = have not. *I haven't seen David today.*

hay NOUN dried grass used as animal feed.

he (him, himself) a man, boy or male animal.

he'd = he had, he would. *He'd come if he could.*

he'll = he will. *He'll do that.*

he's = he is, he has. *He's on his way.*

head NOUN **1** the part of your body above your neck. **2** the person in charge. **3** the front part or top of something.

headache NOUN a pain in your head.

headteacher NOUN the teacher in charge of a school.

did you know?

heart

The heart is about the same size as your clenched fist and lies in the middle of your chest. It is made up of a special kind of muscle, called cardiac muscle, which never gets tired. The heart is constantly at work, pumping blood around your body, so that each cell gets the food and oxygen it needs. It pumps blood around the body about 1,500 times a day.

heal VERB to become healthy again.

health NOUN the condition of your body.

healthy ADJECTIVE (healthier, healthiest) well, without any illness.

hear VERB (heard) **1** to receive sounds through your ears. **2** to get news of, to be told.

heard *See* **hear**. *We heard the news.*

heart NOUN **1** the part of your body that pumps the blood round. **2** a kind of geometric shape. **3** the centre of your feelings. **4** the middle of something.

heat NOUN **1** warmth. **2** a race or competition that comes before the final and decides who will take part in the final.

heat VERB to make something hot.

heavy ADJECTIVE (heavier, heaviest) **1** weighing a lot, difficult to lift. **2** worse or more than usual. *Heavy snow.*

heavy

hedgehog NOUN a small, prickly animal that feeds at night and rolls itself into a ball for protection.

hedgehog

heel NOUN **1** the back part of your foot. **2** the part of your shoe under this.

height NOUN how tall or high something is.

held *See* **hold**. *He held the baby in his arms.*

helicopter NOUN an aircraft with large blades that go round above it instead of wings.

helicopter

hello said when you are greeting someone or when you answer the telephone. *I picked up the telephone and said, 'Hello!'.*

helmet NOUN a hard hat worn to protect the head. Workers on building sites wear helmets to protect them from falling objects.

did you know?

hippopotamus

According to its history, the word *hippopotamus* means 'river horse'. Other English words that have *hippos* include: *hippodrome*, which originally meant 'horse-race' and the name *Philip*, which literally means 'lover of horses'.

help VERB **1** to do something to make things easier for someone else, to assist. **2** to avoid or stop doing something. **3** to serve food and drink.

hen NOUN a female chicken usually kept for laying eggs.

hen

her, herself *See* **she**. *I like her.*

herb NOUN a plant used as a medicine or to make food tastier. *She added some mixed herbs to the stew.*

here in, at or to this place. *You are here.*

hers that or those belonging to her. *The football boots over there are hers.*

hiccup VERB to make little choking sounds in your throat.

hid, hidden *See* **hide**. *Mum has hidden the Easter eggs.*

hide VERB (hiding, hid, hidden) to put out of sight, to keep secret. *'You are hiding something,' she said.*

high ADJECTIVE **1** a long way up from the ground. **2** measuring from top to bottom. **3** very important.

hill NOUN an area of high ground, sloping at the sides. *Climb the hill.*

him, himself *See* **he**. *I like him.*

hippopotamus NOUN (PLURAL hippopotamuses or hippopotami) a big animal with short legs that lives by rivers in Africa.

his belonging to him, that or those belonging to him. *That book is his.*

history NOUN the study of the past.

hit NOUN **1** a blow. **2** a great success.

hit VERB (hitting, hit) to bang hard against something.

herbs

did you know?

holiday

A holiday was originally a 'holy day'. This was a day that was a religious festival, and so people did not have to do their usual work.

hive NOUN a place where bees live.

hive

hobby NOUN (PLURAL hobbies) something that you like to do in your spare time.

hold VERB (held) to have or carry something firmly in your hands or arms.

hole NOUN **1** an opening or gap. **2** an animal's home.

holiday NOUN a time of rest when you are not at school or at work.

hollow ADJECTIVE with an empty space inside, not solid all the way through.

home NOUN **1** the place where you live. **2** a place where people or animals live together so that they can be looked after.

honey NOUN the sweet, sticky food that bees make.

hood NOUN **1** something you cover your head with, often part of a coat or jacket. **2** a folding cover, like that on a pram.

hoof NOUN (PLURAL hoofs or hooves) the foot of an animal such as a horse.

hook NOUN a piece of metal or plastic, curved to catch something, or to hang things on.

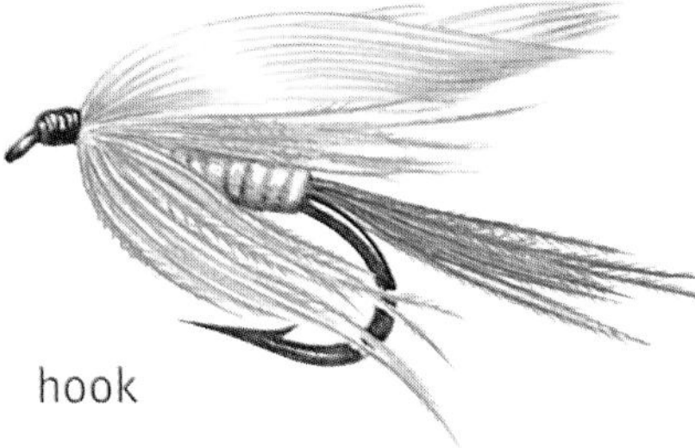
hook

hoop NOUN a large ring of wood, metal, etc.

hop VERB (hopping, hopped) **1** to jump on one foot. **2** to move by jumping along, as some animals and birds do.

hope VERB (hoping, hoped) to wish for something. *I hoped that I would win the race.*

horn NOUN **1** one of the hard, pointed parts that grow on the heads of animals like cows and goats. **2** a musical instrument that you blow into. **3** something on a vehicle that makes a loud noise as a signal or warning.

horrible ADJECTIVE nasty and unpleasant. *She was horrible to me.*

horse NOUN a large animal with a mane and tail that can be ridden or used to pull other vehicles. *Belinda is learning to ride a horse.*

horse

hospital NOUN a place where sick people stay for treatment. *Robert had to stay in hospital for three days.*

hot ADJECTIVE (hotter, hottest) **1** giving off a lot of heat. *Hot sun.* **2** having a burning taste. *The chillies in the soup were extremely hot.*

did you know?

horses

More than 5000 years ago horses were being used in Egypt for riding and pulling chariots and carts.

Until the 1800's the horse was the fastest form of transport. They did all kinds of work, both in towns and in the country, until they were replaced by modern farm machinery and transport.

hotel NOUN a building in which you stay when you are on holiday, where you pay for a room and meals.

hotel

hour NOUN a period of time equal to 60 minutes.

house NOUN a building where usually just one family lives.

house

hovercraft NOUN a vehicle that can move over land and water on a cushion of air.

how 1 in what way. **2** by what amount. **3** in what state.

hug VERB (hugging, hugged) to hold tightly in your arms. *I hugged my teddy bear close as I fell asleep.*

huge ADJECTIVE very large. *It was my birthday, so Mum cut me a huge slice of my favourite cake.*

hum VERB (humming, hummed) **1** to make a sound like a bee buzzing. **2** to sing without opening your lips.

human ADJECTIVE of people. *A human being.*

human NOUN a man, woman or child, a person rather than an animal.

hump NOUN a bump or lump that sticks up.

hump

hundred NOUN the number 100.

hung *See* **hang**. *I hung my coat on the peg.*

hungry ADJECTIVE (hungrier, hungriest) feeling that you want or need food. *I was very hungry after my run.*

hunt VERB **1** to chase wild animals for food or sport. **2** to search for something. *We hunted for my slippers.*

hurry VERB (hurrying, hurried) to move quickly. *I hurried to school because I knew I was late.*

hurt VERB (hurt) to cause pain or harm. *I hurt my knee when I fell off my bike.*

husband NOUN the man that a woman is married to.

Ii

ice-cream

I (me, myself) the speaker or writer himself or herself.

I'd = I had, I would. *I'd seen them.*

I'll = I will. *I'll come later.*

I'm = I am. *I'm very happy.*

I've = I have. *I've an idea.*

ice NOUN frozen water.

ice

did you know?

igloo

Igloo comes from the Inuit language, the language of the people of northern Canada, and parts of Greenland and Alaska.

Other words that come from Inuit which have become part of the English language include *anorak* and *kayak*.

ice-cream NOUN a sweet, creamy, frozen food, often served in a wafer cone.

ice-skating NOUN moving on ice wearing skates.

iceberg NOUN a large mass of ice that floats in the sea.

icicle NOUN a long pointed piece of ice that hangs down from a roof or other surface.

icing NOUN a mixture made from powdered sugar that is used to cover cakes.

idea NOUN a thought or plan in your mind about what to do, how something can be done, etc.

if 1 supposing that. *I'd buy a new car if I could afford it.* **2** whether or not. *Do you know if it's raining?* **3** whenever. *If I don't keep my room tidy, I can't find anything.*

igloo NOUN an Inuit shelter made with blocks of snow.

igloo

idea

ill ADJECTIVE unwell, sick.

illness NOUN a disease or sickness.

imagine VERB (imagining, imagined) to picture something in your mind.

imitate VERB (imitating, imitated) to copy something or someone.

immediately at once, now.

important ADJECTIVE **1** to be taken seriously. **2** valuable. **3** well known.

impossible ADJECTIVE not possible, cannot be done.

in 1 inside. *Your dinner is in the oven.* **2** at. *They live in Manchester.* **3** into. *He jumped in the pool.* **4** during. *In the school holidays.*

indoors inside a building.

information NOUN knowledge about something.

inhaler NOUN a device you use to breathe in medicines.

initial NOUN the first letter of your name.

initial

injection NOUN medicine put into your body with a needle.

injure VERB (injuring, injured) to harm someone. *To injure your leg.*

ink NOUN a coloured liquid that you use with a pen to write or draw.

insect NOUN a small creature with six legs and a body that is divided into three parts.

insect

did you know?

insects

Insects are easily the most numerous of all animal species. Around eight out of ten of all the earth's animals are insects. Man is aware of 850,000 different kinds of insects.

Some insects are helpful to man. Bees, for example, give us honey, and ladybirds prey on aphids which attack many plants. This is useful for gardeners. Other insects can be harmful, such as the mosquito, which can carry the fatal disease malaria.

inside 1 in or near the inner part of something. 2 indoors. *When it rains outside, I always stay inside.*

instead in place of. *I chose to wear the red dress to the party, instead of the blue.*

instruction NOUN some information that tells you what to do. *The instructions on the map showed the way to the treasure.*

instrument

instrument NOUN **1** a tool. **2** something that you play to make music.

interested ADJECTIVE wanting to know more about something. *Harry was interested in astronomy.*

interesting ADJECTIVE something that keeps your attention.

interfere VERB (interfering, interfered) to get involved in a situation that does not concern you.

did you know?

inverted commas

- *Inverted commas* are the punctuation marks (‘ ’) or (“ ”) that are used at the beginning and end of speech when it is written down.
- They are also called *quotation marks.*
- They are always used in pairs, like this:

  ‘Come with me,’ said Nathan.

  “Can I tell you a secret?” whispered Julie.

Internet NOUN a large number of computers all over the world that are linked together to work as a system.

interrupt VERB to break in when someone else is in the middle of doing or saying something. *James rudely interrupted the conversation.*

into in or to the inside. *I stepped into the room.*

invention NOUN something new that has not been made before. The wheel, the telephone and the television were all inventions.

invisible ADJECTIVE not able to be seen.

invitation NOUN something written or spoken to you, asking you to come to a party, meal, etc.

invitation

invite VERB (inviting, invited) to ask someone to come to a party, meal, etc. *I invited all my friends at school to my birthday party.*

invoice NOUN a document asking for payment for goods that have been sent or work that has been done. *He gave me an invoice for £1500.*

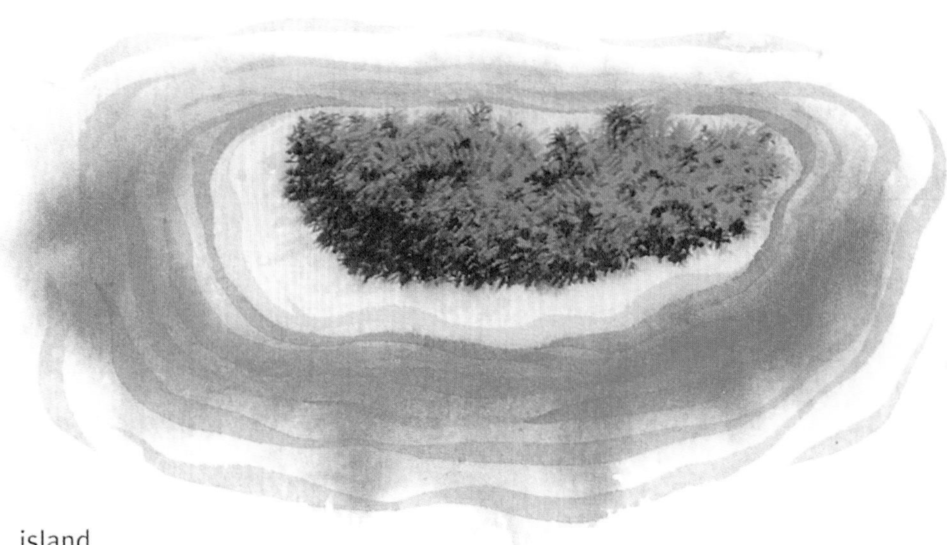

island

iron NOUN **1** a metal used to make steel. **2** a device for getting creases out of clothes.

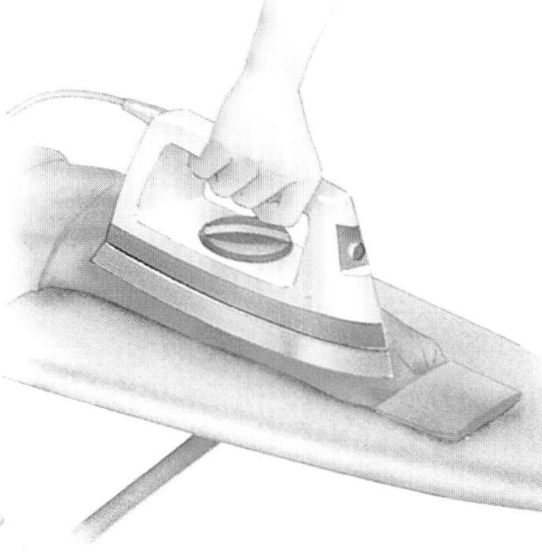

iron

irony NOUN using words to say the very opposite of what they really mean. *'How very clever of you to smash my best dinner plate!'*

irregular ADJECTIVE **1** not regular or usual. *He works irregular hours.* **2** not even or smooth. *The surface of the road was irregular.*

is *See* **be**. *Sally is my best friend.*

island NOUN a piece of land that has water all round it.

isn't = is not. *Ray isn't here.*

it (itself) that thing, situation, etc.

it's = it is, it has. *It's a very nice present.*

itch NOUN a feeling that makes you want to scratch. *I scratched the itch on my nose.*

item NOUN a single thing on a list or in a group of other things. *An item of news.*

its belonging to it. *Its colour.*

ivy NOUN a climbing evergreen plant with shiny, pointed leaves.

ivy

jet

jacket NOUN a short coat.

jagged ADJECTIVE having sharp, rough edges.

jail NOUN a prison.

jail

jam NOUN **1** a sweet food made by boiling fruit with sugar. **2** a mass of things tightly crowded together. *A traffic jam.*

January NOUN the first month of the year.

jar NOUN a glass container that has a lid and a wider mouth than a bottle.

jazz NOUN a kind of music with a strong rhythm.

jealous ADJECTIVE **1** envious, wanting what someone else has. **2** afraid of losing what you have.

jeans PLURAL NOUN strong, casual trousers, often made out of denim cloth.

jelly NOUN a soft, clear dessert that wobbles when you move it.

jellyfish NOUN (PLURAL jellyfish) a sea creature that looks like a jelly and can sting you.

jersey NOUN a sweater, a jumper.

jet NOUN **1** a powerful stream of liquid, gas, etc., forced through a small opening. **2** a kind of aeroplane with jet engines.

January

did you know?

jellyfish

A Portuguese man-of-war is a very large jellyfish.

It has long tentacles, which may be 25 metres long. These tentacles have poisonous stings that can be dangerous to swimmers.

jewel NOUN a precious stone that can be used to decorate valuable ornaments.

jewellery NOUN ornaments like necklaces and rings, made out of precious metals and often decorated with jewels.

jigsaw NOUN a puzzle in which you have to fit together lots of different pieces to make a picture.

jigsaw

job NOUN **1** the regular work that you get paid to do. **2** any piece of work or task.

join VERB **1** to fasten together. **2** to become a member of a group or club.

joke NOUN something funny said to make you laugh.

joke VERB (joking, joked) to say something funny or tell a funny story.

jolly ADJECTIVE happy and cheerful.

journey NOUN the distance you travel to get from one place to another.

jug NOUN a container with a handle and a lip for pouring liquids from.

juice NOUN the liquid in fruit, plants, etc.

July NOUN the seventh month of the year, after June and before August.

July

jump VERB **1** to leap up in the air by pushing off with both your feet. **2** to move suddenly, often because something frightens or surprises you.

jumper NOUN a knitted piece of clothing that you pull over your head to cover the upper part of your body.

June NOUN the sixth month of the year, after May and before July.

jungle NOUN a thick forest in hot countries.

jungle

junk NOUN old things that are not worth very much.

just 1 exactly. *I had just the right money.* **2** almost not. *I just made it in time for lessons.* **3** very recently. *The shop had just closed.* **4** only. *I just wanted to ask you something.*

just ADJECTIVE fair and right. *A just decision.*

justice NOUN **1** treatment that is just, fair and right. **2** a country's system of laws and how they are operated by the law courts. **3** a judge. *A Justice of the Peace.*

June

justify VERB (justifies, justifying, justified) to defend or to prove that something is just and fair.

jut VERB (juts, jutting, jutted) to stick out farther than other things around it, to project. *The balcony juts out from the side of the house.*

did you know?

July

The month of *July* was originally called *Quintilis*, the fifth month, as the Roman year began in March.

Julius Caesar was born in *Quintilis*, but after his death the name of the month was changed to July, in his honour.

The Fourth of July is a very important day for Americans. This is when they celebrate officially gaining their independence from England, on that day in 1776.

July is also an important month for the French. On July 14, 1789, in Paris, the Bastille was captured. This symbolized the end of the French Revolution, when the ordinary people of France gained control over the cruel aristocrats who had been in power before.

A B C D E F G H I J K L M N O P Q R S T U V W X Y Z

Kk

kangaroo

kangaroo NOUN a large Australian animal that has big, strong back legs for jumping and keeps its young in a pouch.

karaoke NOUN entertainment in which people sing along to a backing track while the words appear on a screen.

karate NOUN a Japanese form of self-defence using blows and kicks.

keep VERB (kept) **1** to have something with you that you do not give back. **2** to look after something. **3** to stay or remain. **4** to own.

kennel NOUN a shelter for a dog to live in.

kept *See* **keep**. *We kept the video.*

kerb NOUN the raised edge between the pavement and the road.

kennel

kettle NOUN a metal or plastic container with a handle and a spout for boiling water in.

key NOUN **1** a shaped piece of metal for opening and closing locks. **2** a part of a typewriter or piano that works when you press it with your finger. **3** a set of musical notes. **4** something that explains symbols or abbreviations on a diagram or map.

keyboard NOUN the set of keys that you press to work an instrument like a piano or computer.

kick VERB to hit with your foot. *I kicked the football and it flew straight into the goal.*

kill VERB to cause someone to die.

kilogram NOUN a measurement of weight equal to 1,000 grams or 2.21 pounds.

kilometre NOUN a measurement of length equal to 1,000 metres or 0.62 miles.

kind ADJECTIVE helpful and friendly, doing good to others. *I always try to be kind to my friends.*

kind NOUN sort, type.

king NOUN **1** the male ruler of a country. **2** a chess piece.

did you know?

kangaroos

Kangaroos are marsupials that live in Australia and New Guinea.

In Australia, kangaroos are considered to be a pest and are sometimes hunted.

There are over 50 kinds of kangaroo. The red kangaroo is one of the largest, and may be taller and heavier than a man.

kiss VERB to touch someone with your lips as a greeting, or because you love them. *When my best friend arrived at the party, I gave her a kiss on the cheek.*

kiss

kit NOUN **1** a group of things kept together because they are used for a similar purpose. *A shoe-cleaning kit.* **2** a set of clothing or equipment that you use when you play a sport. *Football kit.* **3** all the bits and pieces that you need to make something. *A model aeroplane kit.*

kitchen NOUN the room where you prepare and cook food.

kite NOUN a light frame covered with paper or material which you hold by a long string and fly in the air on windy days.

kitten NOUN a baby cat.

kittens

knee NOUN the part of your body where your leg bends.

knew *See* **know**. *We knew the answer.*

knickers PLURAL NOUN pants worn by girls and women.

knife NOUN (PLURAL knives) a device with a blade and handle that cuts things.

knit VERB (knitting, knitted or knit) to make wool into clothes by using special needles or a machine.

knives *See* **knife**.

knock VERB to bang against something to make a noise. *I knocked on the door to let them know that I was there.*

knot NOUN **1** the fastening made when you tie two pieces of something together. **2** a hard lump in wood. **3** the way that you measure the speed of a boat.

know VERB (knew, known) **1** to remember or understand something you have learnt. **2** to recognize someone. *I know that I have seen your face before.*

known *See* **know**. *We have known them for years.*

knowledge NOUN the things that you know and understand, things that you learn by study.

knowledgeable ADJECTIVE clever and well-informed about a subject.

know-all NOUN somebody who thinks they know a great deal about everything.

know-how NOUN practical knowledge and ability.

knit

did you know?

We do not say the letter *k* at the beginning of many words which begin with *kn-* on this page: *knee, knickers, knife, knit, knock, knot, know, knuckle*. The *k* is silent and these words all begin with an 'n' sound.

knuckle NOUN the bones at the joint of a finger.

koala NOUN an Australian animal that looks like a small bear. Koalas live in eucalyptus trees and feed on their leaves.

koala

a b c d e f g h i j k l m n o p q r s t u v w x y z

Ll

lamb

label NOUN a piece of paper or card which gives you information about the thing that it is attached to.

lace NOUN **1** delicate cloth with a lot of holes in it. **2** a thin piece of cord that you use to tie shoes and boots.

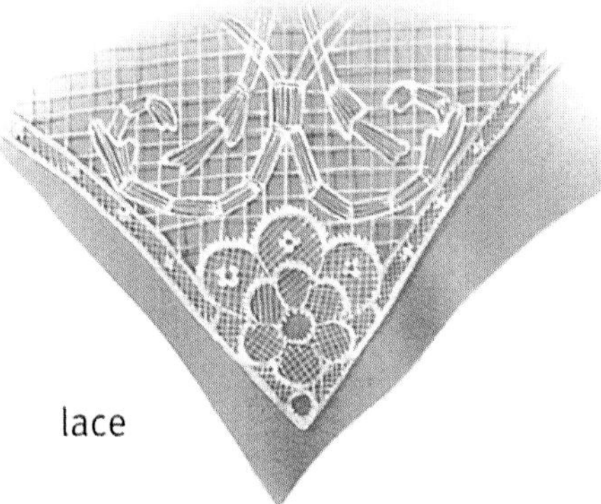
lace

ladder NOUN two long pieces of wood or metal with rungs fixed between them that you use for climbing.

lagoon NOUN a seawater lake separated from the sea by sandbanks or rocks.

laid *See* **lay**. *The hen laid an egg.*

lain *See* **lie**. *They have lain in the sun for too long.*

lake NOUN a large area of water with land all round it.

lamb NOUN **1** a young sheep. **2** meat from a young sheep.

lamp NOUN a device to give light.

land NOUN **1** a country. **2** solid ground, not the sea.

land VERB to come back to solid ground from a ship or an aeroplane.

landing NOUN the floor space at the top of the stairs.

language NOUN the sounds you use to speak or the words you use to write.

lap NOUN **1** the flat area formed by the top of your legs when you sit down. **2** once round a course or track.

lap VERB (lapping, lapped) to drink like a cat does.

did you know?

languages

There are around 3000 languages in the world today. Many animals have ways of communicating, but the spoken word is something that only humans can do so far. Spoken language evolved first and later humans devised a way of writing it down.

large ADJECTIVE big in size or number.

last ADJECTIVE **1** after all the others. *The last train left over an hour ago.* **2** the most recent. *The last time we saw them.*

last VERB to continue for some time.

late ADJECTIVE **1** after the right time. *Late for school.* **2** near the end of a period of time. *Late in the day.*

laugh VERB the sound that you make when you are happy or when you find something funny. *The clowns at the circus always make me laugh.*

law NOUN a rule that the government makes which everyone has to keep.

laugh

lawn NOUN an area of short, mowed grass in a park or garden.

lawn

lawnmower NOUN a machine for cutting grass on lawns.

lay *See* **lie**. *She lay down on the bed.*

lay VERB (laid) **1** to place or set in a particular position. **2** to produce an egg. *I laid the knives and forks on the table, ready for dinner.*

layer NOUN an amount or level of substance that covers a surface.

lazy ADJECTIVE (lazier, laziest) not wanting to do any work. *Mum says I am lazy because I watch television instead of doing my homework.*

lead (said like **bed**) NOUN **1** a soft, grey metal. **2** the black part in the middle of a pencil.

lead (said like **feed**) NOUN **1** the first position in a race or competition. **2** the main part in a play or film. **3** the strap that you tie to a dog's collar to take it for a walk.

lead (said like **feed**) VERB (led) **1** to go in front to show the way. **2** to be in first place. **3** to be in charge.

leader NOUN **1** someone who goes first. **2** the most important person or the one in charge.

leaf NOUN (PLURAL leaves) the flat, green part of a plant that grows from a stem or branch. Some leaves change colour in autumn.

leaves

lean VERB (leant or leaned) **1** to be in a sloping position. **2** to support yourself by resting against something.

leant or **leaned** *See* **lean**. *Jo leant against the wall.*

learn VERB (learnt or learned) to study to get knowledge, to find out about things. *I would like to learn to speak French.*

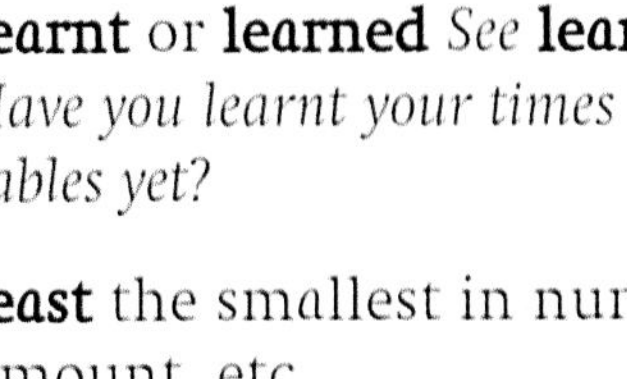

learnt or **learned** *See* **learn**. *Have you learnt your times tables yet?*

least the smallest in number, amount, etc.

leather NOUN material made from animal skins.

leave VERB (leaving, left) **1** to go away from. **2** to put something in a place where it stays.

leaves *See* leaf.

led VERB *Harry led the way.*

left *See* **leave**. *Tom left the house very early in the morning.*

left ADJECTIVE to or on the opposite side or direction to right.

did you know?

learn

The word *school* comes from the ancient Greek word *schole*, which means leisure.

The ancient Greeks thought that learning should be fun; something to do in your spare time!

did you know?

legends

In the legends of King Arthur he and his knights met at a round table that was large enough to seat 150 people.

It is said that the significance of the round table was to show that all of the knights were of equal importance.

leg NOUN **1** the part of your body between your hips and your feet that you use to walk with. **2** the part that supports a piece of furniture.

legend NOUN an old, well-known story that may or may not be true. *The legend of King Arthur.*

leggings PLURAL NOUN tight-fitting, stretchy trousers.

lemon NOUN a sour, yellow fruit.

lemon

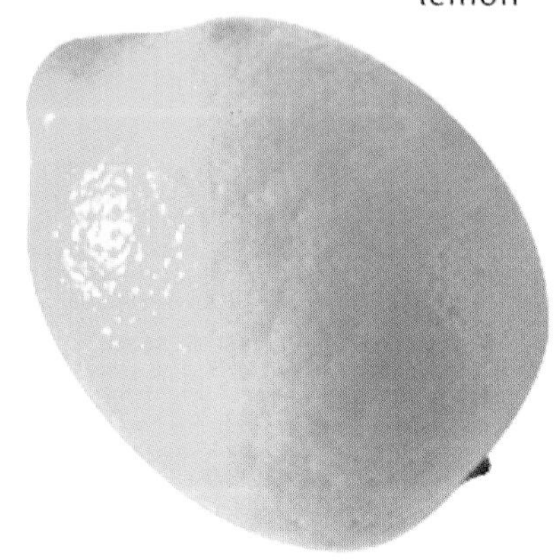

lend VERB (lent) to let someone use something for a period of time.

length NOUN the measurement of something from end to end.

lent *See* **lend**. *I've lent my book.*

leotard

leopard NOUN a wild animal of the cat family with yellow fur and black spots.

leotard NOUN a tight-fitting, stretchy body suit that you wear for exercise or dancing.

did you know?

leotard

The leotard is named after the French acrobat Jules Léotard (1842–70), who designed and introduced the original costume for the circus.

He was one of France's most famous acrobats and was known as 'That Daring Young Man on the Flying Trapeze'.

less a smaller amount, not so much.

lesson NOUN a period in the school day when a subject is taught.

let's = let us. *Let's go.*

letter NOUN **1** a message written on paper that you send to someone in an envelope, usually through the post. **2** one of the signs you write to make words.

lettuce NOUN a green plant eaten in salads.

lettuce

level ADJECTIVE **1** flat and smooth. **2** even or equal

library NOUN (PLURAL libraries) a building where books are kept for you to borrow and read.

lick VERB to touch something with your tongue.

lid NOUN the cover of a container.

lie NOUN something you say which you know is not the truth.

lie VERB (lying, lied) to tell a lie.

did you know?

library

The first major library in the world was the Library of Alexandria in Egypt. It was founded in the 3rd century BC and at its largest may have contained more than 700,000 books and other items.

lighthouse

lie VERB (lying, lay, lain) to be in a flat position, as when you are in bed. *We can lie on our backs and look at the stars.*

life NOUN (PLURAL lives) **1** being alive and breathing. **2** the time between birth and death. **3** the way you live or spend your time.

lifeboat NOUN a boat that rescues people who are in danger at sea.

lift NOUN **1** a large metal box on pulleys used to carry people from one floor of a building to another. **2** a free ride in a vehicle.

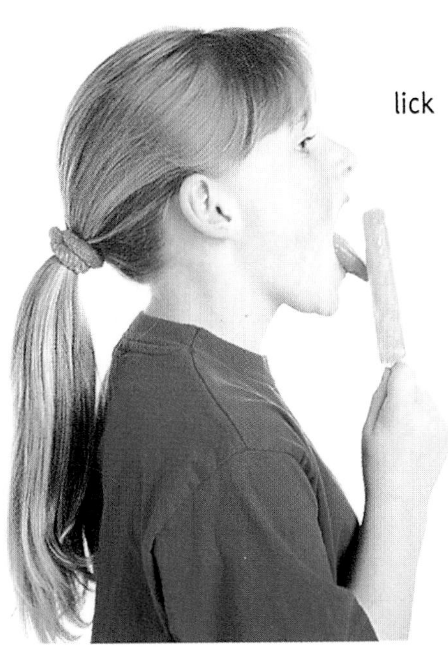
lick

lift VERBto pick something up and place it in a higher position.

light ADJECTIVE not heavy.

light NOUN **1** brightness from the sun or a lamp that lets you see things. **2** something which gives out light.

light bulb NOUN glass part of an electric light or lamp that gives out light.

lighthouse NOUN tall tower on the coast that flashes a light to warn ships of danger.

lightning NOUN flash of light in the sky in a storm.

like VERB (liking, liked) **1** to be fond of someone or something. **2** to wish.

like 1 similar to. **2** for example.

likely ADJECTIVE (likelier, likeliest) **1** expected. **2** suitable.

line NOUN **1** long, thin mark. *Draw a line on the blackboard.* **2** a piece of string, wire, etc. *A washing-line.* **3** a row, queue. *A line of cars.*

lightning

lion

loaf

litter

lion NOUN wild animal of the cat family.

lips PLURAL NOUN the pink edges of your mouth.

liquid NOUN anything that is not solid and flows like water.

list NOUN a number of things written down one below the other.

listen VERB to pay attention to sounds that you hear.

litre NOUN a measurement of liquid equal to 1.759 pints.

did you know?

litre

The word *litre* was originally the unit of money used in Sicily. It then came into French where it was used as a unit of capacity (how much a container holds), but it became used less and less.

It was revived at the end of the 18th century as the basic metric measure of capacity.

litter NOUN **1** rubbish. **2** a family of baby animals all born at the same time.

little ADJECTIVE small, not large in size or amount.

live VERB (living, lived) **1** to be alive. **2** to make your home in a particular place. **3** to spend your life in a particular way.

lives *See* **life**.

living room NOUN room in a home to sit and relax in.

loaf NOUN (PLURAL loaves) bread shaped and baked in one piece.

loaves *See* **loaf**.

lock NOUN **1** a device that fastens something when you use it with a key. **2** a section of a canal with gates at either end, to move boats between different water levels.

lock VERB to fasten something with a key.

loft NOUN the space in the roof of a house.

log NOUN a thick piece of wood cut from a tree.

lonely ADJECTIVE (lonelier, loneliest) feeling sad because you are on your own or you do not have any friends. *I felt very lonely when we first moved.*

long ADJECTIVE **1** covering a great distance or time. **2** the measurement of something from one end to the other. *The boat is twenty metres long.*

look VERB **1** to see with your eyes. **2** to appear or seem.

loose ADJECTIVE **1** not tight. **2** free.

lorry NOUN (PLURAL lorries) a large vehicle for carrying goods, a truck.

lose VERB (losing, lost) **1** to misplace something. **2** to be beaten in a competition or game.

lost *See* **lose**. *We lost the football match.*

lot NOUN a large number or amount.

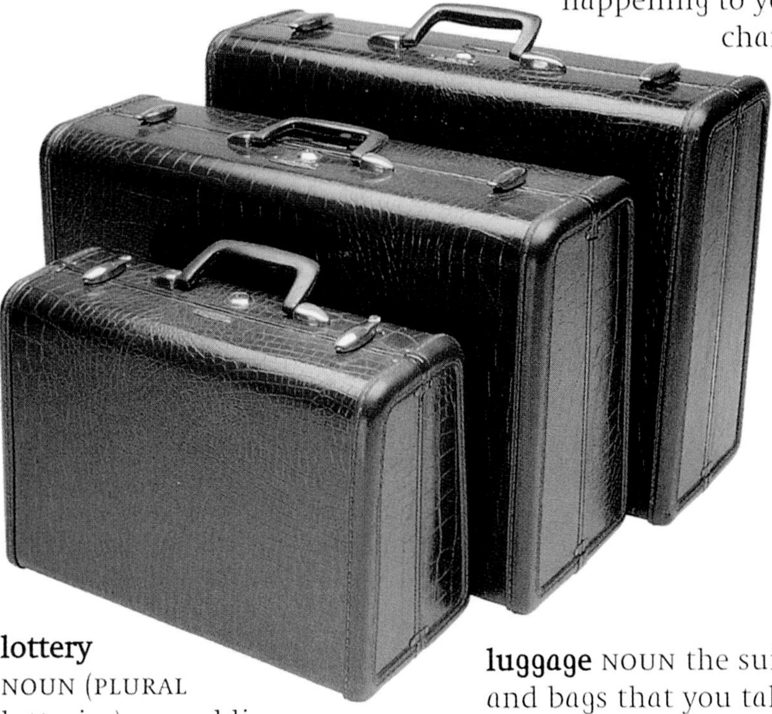

luggage

lottery NOUN (PLURAL lotteries) a gambling game in which you buy a ticket with certain numbers in the hope of winning prizes.

loud ADJECTIVE noisy.

loudspeaker NOUN a device that produces the sound in radios, music systems, etc.

lounge NOUN room in a home to sit and relax in.

love NOUN a very strong feeling of liking for someone. *I love you.*

love VERB (loving, loved) to like someone or something very strongly.

lovely ADJECTIVE (lovelier, loveliest) **1** beautiful. *A lovely face.* **2** nice, pleasant. *We had a lovely time on holiday.*

low ADJECTIVE near to the ground, not high.

lucky ADJECTIVE (luckier, luckiest) having good things happening to you by chance.

luggage NOUN the suitcases and bags that you take with you on a journey.

lump NOUN **1** a solid mass of something. **2** a swelling.

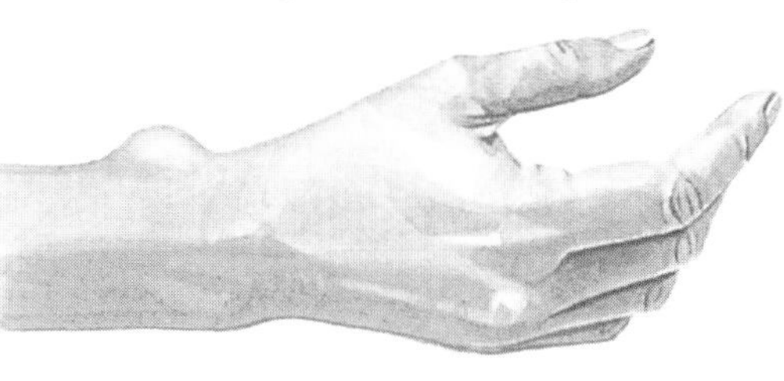

lump

lunch NOUN the meal you eat in the middle of the day. *We went out for lunch and then shopped in the afternoon.*

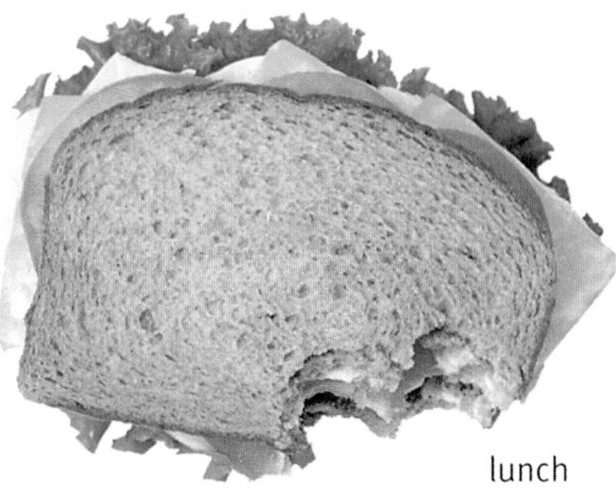

lunch

lung NOUN one of the two organs inside your chest that you use for breathing. The lungs take in oxygen from the air and give out carbon dioxide.

lunge VERB to make a sudden thrust forward. *She lunged at him with a stick.*

lure VERB to attract and tempt, to lead astray. *They were lured by the bright lights of the fair.*

lurk VERB to wait around out of sight with a dishonest purpose, to prowl. *There is somebody lurking under the trees.*

did you know?

lung

Most kinds of fish can only breathe underwater, using gills to take in oxygen. The lungfish is the only type of fish which also has lungs to help it to breathe in the swamps where it lives. When there is too little oxygen, the lungfish can survive for up to half an hour between trips to the surface of the water to take a breath!

Mm

March

macaroni NOUN short, thin tubes of pasta.

machine NOUN a piece of equipment that uses power to work.

made *See* **make**. *Made in England.*

magazine NOUN a regular publication in a paper cover that contains stories, pictures, advertisements, etc.

magic NOUN **1** conjuring tricks. **2** using witchcraft to try to control what happens.

magic

magician NOUN a person who does conjuring tricks.

magnet NOUN a piece of metal that draws other metal objects towards it.

main ADJECTIVE most important.

make VERB (making, made) **1** to produce or build something. **2** to cause something to happen. **3** to earn or get.

male NOUN a person or animal belonging to the sex that cannot produce babies or young.

mammal NOUN an animal that drinks milk from its mother's body.

man NOUN (PLURAL men) an adult male.

many (more, most) a large number. *Many schools.*

map NOUN a drawing that shows countries, rivers, towns, roads, etc.

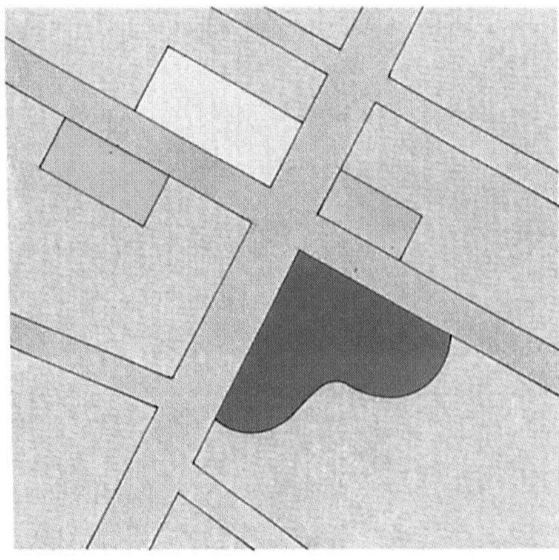
map

marble NOUN **1** a hard stone used for buildings and statues. **2** a small glass ball used to play the game of marbles.

March NOUN the third month of the year, after February and before April.

march VERB to walk with regular strides as soldiers do.

did you know?

macaroni

The word *macaroni* comes originally from Italian. Other words from Italian that have become part of the English language include: *balcony, bandit, cameo, carnival, cartoon, casino, duet, extravaganza, fiasco, gondola, infantry, lava, malaria, paparazzi, piano, pizza, spaghetti, squadron, stiletto, studio, umbrella, violin, volcano.*

mark NOUN **1** a spot or pattern on something, often spoiling it. **2** a number or letter on a piece of work that shows how good it is.

mark VERB **1** to damage a surface by leaving a stain, etc., on it. **2** to put a number or letter on a piece of work that shows how good it is.

market NOUN a place where people buy and sell things from stalls.

marmalade NOUN jam made with oranges.

marry VERB (marrying, married) **1** to become the husband or wife of someone. **2** to join a man and a woman together as husband and wife.

mascara NOUN make-up that you put on your eyelashes to thicken or colour them.

mask NOUN something that you put over your face as a disguise or to protect it.

may VERB (might) **1** to be likely. *I may go out tonight.* **2** to ask if you can do something. *May I leave the room?*

me *See* **I**. *She saw me.*

meal NOUN the food that you eat at a certain time.

mean ADJECTIVE **1** not willing to spend much money. **2** unkind.

matches

match NOUN (PLURAL matches) **1** a short stick with one end coated so that it catches fire when you strike it. **2** a contest between two teams or players.

material NOUN **1** anything that you can make things from. **2** cloth.

mathematics PLURAL NOUN the study of numbers and shapes.

matter NOUN **1** the material from which the universe and everything in it is made. **2** trouble or pain. *What's the matter?*

May NOUN the fifth month of the year, after April and before June.

mean VERB (meant) **1** to show or indicate. *What does this word mean?* **2** to want or intend to do or say something. *I meant to choose this book, not that one.* **3** designed for a particular use. *This toy isn't meant for babies.*

May

meant *See* **mean**. *I meant to come earlier, but I forgot about the time.*

measles NOUN an infectious disease that gives you a temperature and red spots on your skin.

measure VERB (measuring, measured) to find out how long something is, how much it weighs, etc.

measurement NOUN the length, width, height, etc., of something.

meat NOUN the food that we eat that comes from an animal's flesh.

medal NOUN a small piece of metal with a special design on it, awarded to winners of sporting events or to people who have been very brave. *Gary won a medal.*

medicine

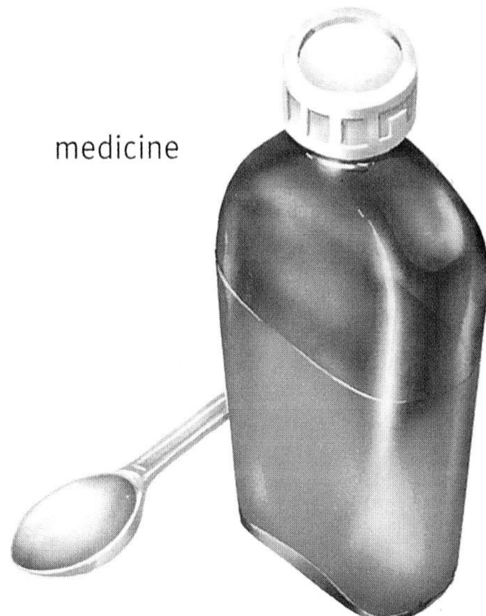

medicine NOUN a liquid or pills that you take when you are ill to make you better. *When I have a cold, medicine always makes me feel better.*

medium ADJECTIVE neither large nor small.

meet VERB (met) to come together with someone.

melt VERB to change something from a solid to a liquid.

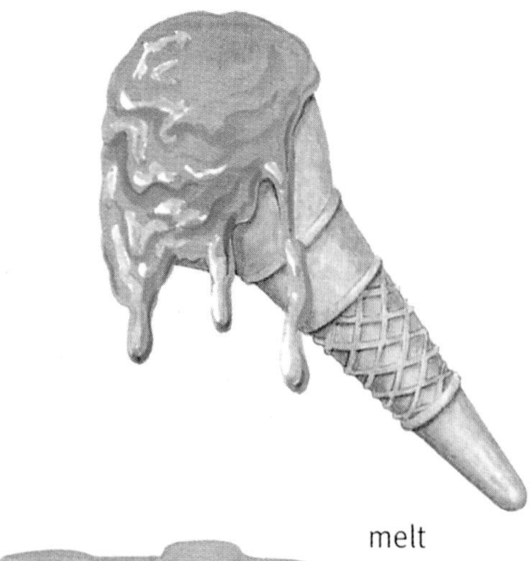
melt

memory NOUN (PLURAL memories) your ability to remember things.

men *See* **man**.

mend VERB to put something back in its proper condition, so that it works again or is not damaged.

merry-go-round NOUN a fairground ride.

mess NOUN an untidy or dirty condition.

message NOUN written or spoken information sent from one person to another.

met *See* **meet**. *We met at the station.*

metal NOUN a hard material like copper, tin, iron or gold.

did you know?

miaow

The word *miaow* is a written imitation of a sound, called *onomatopoeia* (said: on-a-matter-pier). This means that words are formed from natural sounds and to suggest a sound.

Other examples are: *buzz*, *cock-a-doodle-doo*, *crackle*, *crunch*, *cuckoo*, and *ping*.

metre NOUN measurement of length equal to 39.37 inches.

miaow VERB to make a noise like a cat. *When our cat is happy it 'miaows'.*

mice *See* **mouse**.

microscope NOUN an instrument that you look through which makes very small objects appear bigger.

microwave NOUN **1** a short-length electromagnetic wave. **2** an oven that cooks food quickly by using microwaves instead of heat.

midday NOUN 12 o'clock in the daytime.

mirror
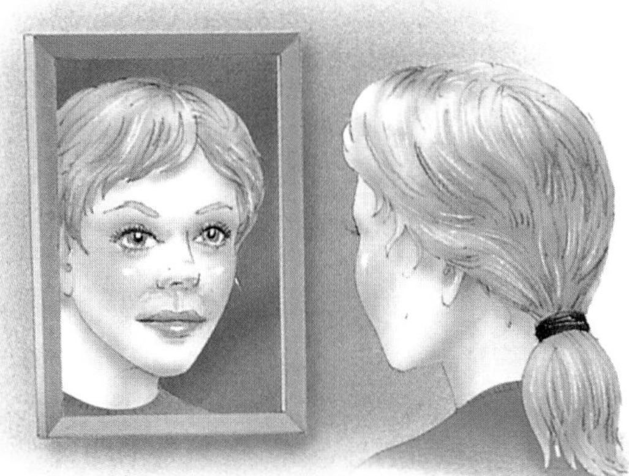

middle NOUN the point that is at an equal distance from either of the two ends or edges of something.

midnight NOUN 12 o'clock at night.

might *See* **may**. *I might have won.*

milk NOUN a white liquid that comes from cows and other female animals, and can be drunk or made into butter and cheese.

millennium NOUN (PLURAL millenniums or millennia) **1** the year 2000. **2** the thousand years beginning in 2000, or more exactly 2001.

million NOUN the number 1,000,000.

mind NOUN your ability to think and feel.

mind VERB to be annoyed or bothered. *I do not mind.*

mine that or those belonging to me. *My sister wanted to keep the trousers, but I told her they were mine.*

minister NOUN **1** someone in charge of a government department. **2** a member of the clergy in the Christian church.

minus NOUN the sign – used when you take away one number from another.

minute NOUN a measurement of time equal to 60 seconds.

mirror NOUN a piece of glass that you can see your reflection in.

Miss a title that you use before the name of an unmarried woman when you are speaking or writing to or about her.

miss VERB **1** to fail to catch, meet, etc., someone or something. **2** to feel sad because you are apart from someone or something.

mist NOUN thin cloud close to the ground.

mistake NOUN something that you do or think that is wrong.

mix VERB to stir or shake different things together so that they cannot be separated again.

mixture NOUN several different things mixed together.

mixture

mobile phone NOUN a telephone without wires that you can carry with you and use wherever you are.

monkey

model NOUN **1** a small copy of something. **2** someone whose job is to wear and show off the latest fashions. **3** a particular version of something.

modern ADJECTIVE of the present time, not old. *We live in a modern house.*

moment NOUN a very short period of time. *It will only take a moment.*

Monday NOUN the day of the week after Sunday and before Tuesday.

money NOUN the coins and notes that you use to buy things.

mongoose NOUN (PLURAL mongooses) a small African or Asian animal with a long body known for its ability to kill poisonous snakes.

mongrel NOUN a dog that is a mixture of different breeds.

monitor NOUN the display screen in a computer system.

monk NOUN a member of a religious community of men who live, pray and work together in a building called a monastery.

monkey NOUN an animal with a long tail that climbs trees.

month NOUN one of the twelve periods of time that the year is divided into, about four weeks.

moon NOUN the small planet that goes round the earth and that you can see in the sky at night.

moon

monster NOUN a large ugly creature in stories.

more *See* **many**, **much**. *More sweets.*

morning NOUN the part of the day between dawn and noon.

mosaic NOUN a picture or design made from pieces of coloured glass or stone.

moss NOUN (PLURAL mosses) a green plant that forms a soft covering on stones in damp places.

most *See* **many**, **much**. *Most children.*

moth NOUN an insect that looks like a butterfly and is active at night.

mother NOUN a woman who has a child.

motor NOUN an engine.

motorbike NOUN two-wheeled vehicle with an engine.

motorway NOUN a wide road that is built for fast travel over a long distance.

mountain NOUN a very high hill with steep sides.

mouse NOUN (PLURAL mice) **1** small, furry animal with a long tail and quick movements, often regarded as a pest. **2** device you use with a computer instead of a keyboard.

mouth NOUN the part of your face through which you speak and into which you put food when you eat.

move VERB (moving, moved) **1** to go from place to place. **2** to put something that was in one place or position into a different one.

Mr a title that you use before a man's name when you are speaking or writing to or about him.

Mrs a title that you use before the name of a married woman when you are speaking or writing to or about her.

Ms a title that you use before the name of a woman when you are speaking or writing to or about her.

much (more, most) a large amount. *How much money do you have?*

mud NOUN soil that is wet and sticky.

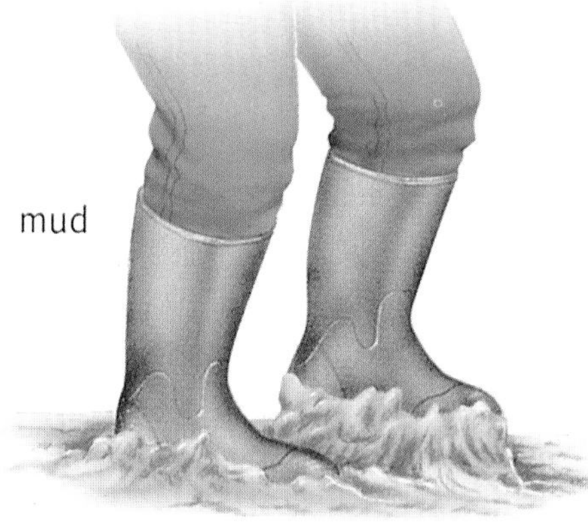

mug NOUN something that you drink out of that has straight sides and is deeper than a cup.

multiply VERB (multiplying, multiplied) **1** to add a number to itself a certain number of times. **2** to increase.

mum, mummy NOUN (PLURAL mums, mummies) a name that a child calls its mother.

mumps NOUN an infectious disease that makes your neck swollen and sore.

muscle NOUN one of the elastic parts inside your body that work to help you to move.

museum NOUN a building where you can go and see interesting things that are often old and valuable.

mushroom NOUN a plant with a short stem and a round top that you can eat, a fungus.

music NOUN **1** sounds arranged in a pattern for people to sing or play on musical instruments. **2** the sheets of paper that these sounds are written down on.

must VERB **1** to have to do something. *I must be home in time for tea.* **2** to be sure or likely to. *You must be pleased with your exam results.*

mustard NOUN a hot-tasting yellow paste made from the seeds of the mustard plant.

mute ADJECTIVE not speaking, dumb.

my belonging to me.

myself *See* **I**. *I can dress myself.*

mystery NOUN (PLURAL mysteries) something not known about or very difficult to understand.

A B C D E F G H I J K L M N O P Q R S T U V W X Y Z

Nn

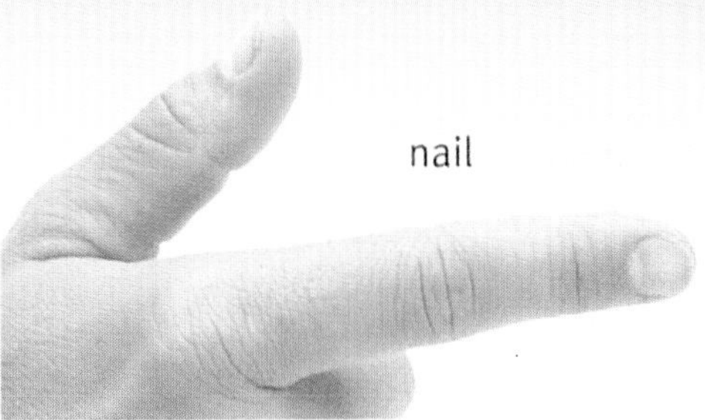
nail

nail NOUN **1** the hard, top part at the end of your finger or toe. **2** short, thin piece of metal, pointed at one end and blunt at the other which is hammered into things to hold them together.

name NOUN the word that someone or something is called by.

narrow

narrow ADJECTIVE not wide, thin.

nasty ADJECTIVE (nastier, nastiest) horrible, unpleasant.

natural ADJECTIVE **1** not man-made. **2** normal.

nature NOUN the things in the world that are not made by people, like plants, the sea, weather, etc.

naughty ADJECTIVE (naughtier, naughtiest) behaving badly.

navy
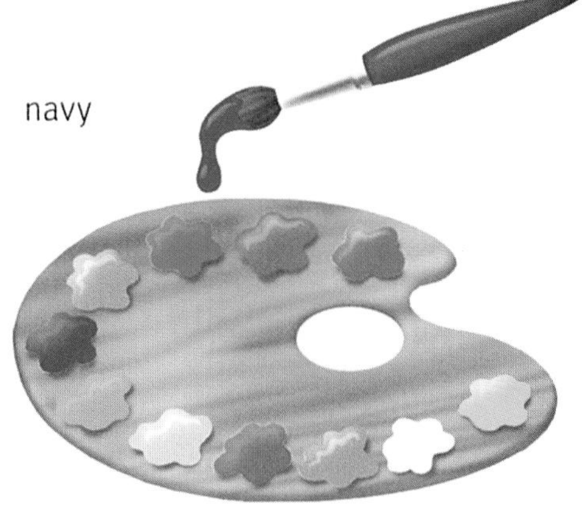

navy NOUN (PLURAL navies) a country's armed forces that fight at sea.

navy ADJECTIVE a dark blue colour.

near close by, not far away from.

nearly almost, not quite.

neat ADJECTIVE tidy.

neck NOUN the part of your body between your head and your shoulders.

necklace NOUN a piece of jewellery that you wear round your neck.

necklace

did you know?

name

Many plants are named because they look like something else. For example, *dandelion*, which comes from the french *dents de lion*, meaning lion's teeth. The flower is jagged like teeth.

need VERB **1** to lack something necessary. *I need a new coat.* **2** to have to do something. *I need to wash my hands.*

needle NOUN a very thin, pointed piece of metal used for injections, sewing, etc.

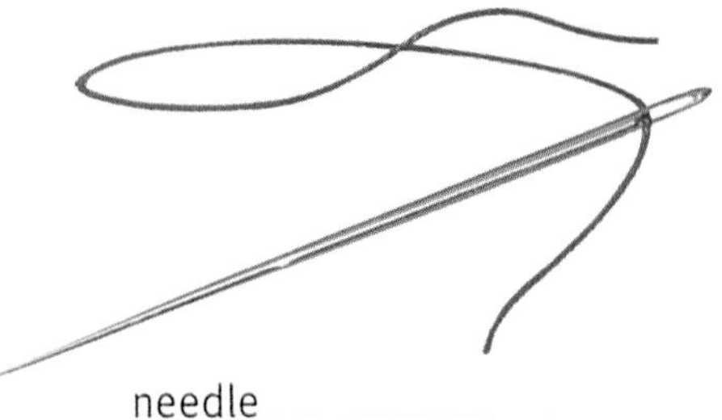
needle

neighbour NOUN someone who lives very near to you.

neither not either of two people or things.

nephew NOUN the son of your brother or sister.

nervous ADJECTIVE worried and frightened about something.

nest

nest NOUN a place where a bird lays its eggs.

net NOUN **1** see-through material made by weaving threads together with equal spaces in between. **2** anything made from this. *A fishing-net.*

night

netball NOUN a team game in which goals are scored by throwing a large ball through a ring on a high post.

never not ever, at no time.

new ADJECTIVE **1** recently made, not experienced or seen before. **2** not used by anyone before.

news NOUN **1** information about things that are happening. **2** a broadcast of this on the television or radio.

newsagent NOUN someone who sells newspapers and magazines.

newspaper NOUN a daily or weekly publication of news printed on a number of sheets of paper that are folded together.

next ADJECTIVE following straight after, nearest.

nibble VERB (nibbling, nibbled) to eat by taking tiny bites.

nice ADJECTIVE pleasant, attractive or enjoyable.

niece NOUN the daughter of your brother or sister.

night NOUN the time of day when it is dark.

nightie NOUN a kind of dress worn by women or girls to go to bed in.

nightmare NOUN a bad and frightening dream.

nine the number 9.

nineteen the number 19.

ninety the number 90.

9

no 1 a word used when you answer someone to disagree with them, refuse them or to say that something is not true. **2** not any. *The refugees had no food.*

nobody, no one no person.

nod VERB (nodding, nodded) to bow your head as a greeting or as a sign that you agree with something.

noise NOUN a sound, usually loud and unpleasant.

noisy ADJECTIVE (noisier, noisiest) making a loud, unpleasant noise.

none not a single one.

noodles PLURAL NOUN very thin strips of pasta.

noodles

noon NOUN 12 o'clock midday.

normal ADJECTIVE usual, ordinary.

did you know?

newspaper

The first newspaper was printed in the 1400's soon after printing began.

A newspaper is exactly what its name suggests, and gives the people who live in a particular place the latest news about what is happening in their local area and also in faraway places.

north NOUN one of the four points of the compass, the direction that is on your left when you face the rising sun.

north

nose NOUN the part of your face above your mouth through which you breathe and smell.

not a word you use to make something that you say or write have the opposite meaning.

note NOUN **1** a short, written message. **2** a piece of paper money. **3** a single musical sound.

nothing not any thing.

notice VERB (noticing, noticed) to feel or observe something.

nought NOUN nothing, the figure 0 or zero.

November NOUN the eleventh month of the year, after October and before December.

November

now at this moment, at present.

nugget NOUN **1** a lump of gold, or anything small and valuable. **2** food shaped into small pieces. *Chicken nuggets.*

nuisance NOUN someone or something that annoys you or causes you problems.

number NOUN **1** a word or figure showing an amount. *6 is an even number.* **2** a word or figure used to name a series of things. *House numbers.* **3** the series of digits that you use to telephone someone. *Do you have my number?*

nun NOUN a member of a religious community of women who live, pray and work together in a building called a convent or abbey.

nurse NOUN someone whose job is to look after sick people or young children.

nursery NOUN (PLURAL nurseries) **1** a place where young children are looked after. **2** a place that grows and sells plants.

nuts

nursery rhyme NOUN a short, simple poem that children like to recite.

nut NOUN **1** a dry fruit or seed inside a hard shell. **2** a piece of metal with a hole in the middle for screwing onto a bolt.

did you know?

noun

- The name of a thing is called a *noun*.
- There are different kinds of noun.
- A *proper noun* is the name of a particular person or thing. Your name is a proper noun. The names of places are also proper nouns.

  Examples of proper nouns are: *William Shakespeare, France, London, Queen Elizabeth.*
- All other nouns are called *common nouns*, for example: book, child, rice.
- *Concrete nouns* are the names given to things that you can see or touch, for example: *book, child, dog. Abstract nouns* are the names given to feelings, qualities or ideas, for example: *surprise, happiness, beauty.*

nutcracker NOUN an instrument for cracking the shells of nuts.

nutritious ADJECTIVE nourishing and good for you as food. *A nutritious meal.*

nylon NOUN strong, man-made cloth. *Tights and stockings are made from nylon.*

Oo

octopus

o'clock the way that you say what the hour is when telling the time. *I go to bed at 7 o'clock.*

oak NOUN a large tree that produces acorns.

oar NOUN a long paddle used to row a boat.

obey VERB to do what someone tells you to do. *We have trained our dog to obey us when we tell her to sit.*

object NOUN a thing. Books, chairs, cups and desks are all objects.

ocean NOUN **1** the sea. **2** a very large sea. *The Atlantic Ocean.*

O

October NOUN the tenth month of the year, after September and before November.

October

octopus NOUN (PLURAL octopuses) a sea creature with eight legs.

odd ADJECTIVE **1** strange, weird. **2** not matching, spare. *An odd sock.* **3** of various kinds. *Odd jobs.* **4** that does not divide exactly by two. *1, 3 and 5 are odd numbers.*

of 1 from the whole of a thing. *A piece of bread.* **2** containing. *A collection of books.* **3** belonging to. *The home of the pop star.* **4** about, to do with. *News of the wedding.*

off 1 no longer on. *My button's come off.* **2** away from a place or position. *The thief ran off.* **3** not working or in use. *The lights were off.*

offer VERB **1** to hold out something for someone to take. *He offered me a chocolate.* **2** to be willing to do something for someone. *We offered to wash up.* **3** to suggest a price that you would pay for something. *I'll offer a good price for the car.*

did you know?

octopus

The octopus is a soft-bodied mollusc that lives in the sea. They are said to be the most intelligent invertebrates (animals with no backbone). They have eight tentacles which they use to pull their victims, such as crabs and shellfish, towards their mouths.

office NOUN **1** a place of business where people work at desks. **2** a government department. *The Office of Fair Trading.*

often many times. *We often go to the park after school, if the weather is warm.*

oil NOUN a thick liquid used as a fuel, to make machines run more easily or for cooking with.

old

old ADJECTIVE **1** not new or young. *My Grandfather says that he is old.* **2** used when referring to the age of someone or something. *The car is three years old.*

on 1 on top of. *The jug is on the shelf.* **2** by or near. *The shop on the corner.* **3** about, to do with. *The lesson on safety in the home.* **4** attached to. *The picture on the wall.* **5** working, in use. *Is the oven on?*

once 1 one time only. *I only ever tried smoking once.* **2** one time in a period of time. *I buy sweets once a week.* **3** some time ago. *Once there were fields where now there are houses.* **4** (at once) immediately.

one 1 the number 1. **2** (oneself) a single person or thing, any person.

oneself *See* **one**. *To behave oneself.*

onion NOUN a round, white vegetable that has a strong taste and smell and a brown papery skin that you peel off.

onion

only 1 no one or nothing else. *I'm the only one who can control the dog.* **2** no more than. *Only three minutes before the bell.* **3** but. *I want to go, only I can't.*

onto to a position on.

open VERB **1** to remove a cover from something. **2** to be ready for business.

open ADJECTIVE **1** not shut. *An open box.* **2** not closed in. *In the open air.* **3** not covered over. *An open-top car.* **4** spread out. *Open hands.*

did you know?

orchestra

In ancient Greece the word *orkhestra* was used to describe the semi-circular space at the front of a stage in a theatre. This space was where the chorus sang and danced, the Greek word *orkheisthai* meaning 'to dance'. English took over the word from Greek via Latin. It was not until the 18th century that the word was used to describe the part of the theatre where the musicians played, and then the group of musicians themselves.

operation NOUN treatment for a patient by cutting their body open to take away, replace or mend a damaged or diseased part.

opposite 1 as different as possible, furthest away from. **2** facing.

or used to show that there is a choice between alternatives.

orange NOUN **1** a sweet juicy round fruit that you peel to eat. **2** a drink made from, or tasting like, oranges.

orange ADJECTIVE the colour of oranges, between red and yellow.

orange

orchard NOUN a field where fruit trees grow.

orchard

orchestra NOUN a group of musicians playing different instruments together.

order NOUN **1** a command. *Orders must be obeyed.* **2** the way things are arranged. *The dictionary is in alphabetical order.* **3** tidiness. *Put your desk in order.* **4** a request to provide something. *May I take your order for lunch?* **5** right behaviour. *The police restored law and order.*

order VERB **1** to tell people what to do. **2** to ask to be provided with something.

ordinary ADJECTIVE not unusual, normal. *He wore his ordinary clothes to his brother's party.*

organ NOUN a large musical instrument usually found in churches. Its long metal pipes make different sounds when air passes through them.

ostrich

ostrich NOUN a large African bird with long legs and a long neck that is unable to fly.

other different from the ones that you have just mentioned.

otter NOUN an animal with thick fur that eats fish and is good at swimming.

our belonging to us.

ourselves *See* **we**. *We saw ourselves on the video.*

did you know?

ostrich

A person who does not accept facts or reality is sometimes likened to an ostrich. This comes from the popular belief that ostriches, when chased, bury their heads in the sand. They think that if they cannot see anything, then they themselves cannot be seen by their pursuers.

out 1 away from, not in. *Out of the bath.* **2** not at home. *My parents are out.* **3** no longer in a game. *The captain was out.* **4** not lit. *The fire's out.*

outdoors outside, in the open air.

outside 1 in a position furthest from the middle. **2** not inside a building.

ought VERB to be the right thing to do. *You ought to go to the doctor.*

oval ADJECTIVE egg-shaped.

oven NOUN a cooker that you use to roast or bake food.

oven

over 1 above, covering. *A mist lay over the fields.* **2** on or to the other side of. *Over the road.* **3** finished, at an end. *The holidays are over.* **4** downwards from an upright position. *The toddler fell over.*

owe VERB (owing, owed) **1** to have to pay. *I owe my mum £5.* **2** to be thankful for something someone else has done. *They owed their lives to the courage of the lifeboat crew.*

owl NOUN bird of prey that hunts at night.

owl

own 1 belonging to you and to no one else. **2** (on your own) alone, by yourself.

own VERB to have, to possess. *I own a car.*

ox NOUN (PLURAL oxen) a bull that is used in some countries for pulling carts, ploughs, etc.

oxygen NOUN a colourless, tasteless gas that makes up about a fifth of the earth's atmosphere. *All life on Earth needs oxygen to live.*

oyster NOUN an edible sea creature that lives inside two shells. *Some oysters produce a pearl inside their shells.*

ozone NOUN a gas that is a form of oxygen but has three atoms instead of two.

Pp

paint

pack VERB **1** to wrap things up or put them into boxes, bags, etc. **2** to crowd tightly together. *Packed into the room.*

package NOUN a small parcel.

packet NOUN a small parcel.

paddle VERB (paddling, paddled) **1** to take your shoes and socks off so that you can walk in shallow water. **2** to move a boat through water with an oar.

page NOUN one side of a piece of paper in a book, magazine, etc.

paid *See* **pay**. *He paid by cheque.*

pain NOUN the feeling you suffer in your body when you have been hurt or you are ill.

paint NOUN a liquid that you brush onto something to colour it.

did you know?

panic

According to the history of the word, *panic* means a strong feeling of fear brought on by the god *Pan*. To the ancient Greeks Pan was the god of woods, shepherds and flocks. He was known for suddenly appearing from trees and bushes and so inspiring 'panic' on those walking by.

paint VERB **1** to colour a wall, ceiling, etc., with paint. **2** to make a picture using paints.

painting NOUN a picture done with paints.

pair NOUN **1** two similar things that go together. *A pair of shoes.* **2** a single thing made up of two similar parts joined together. *A pair of tights.*

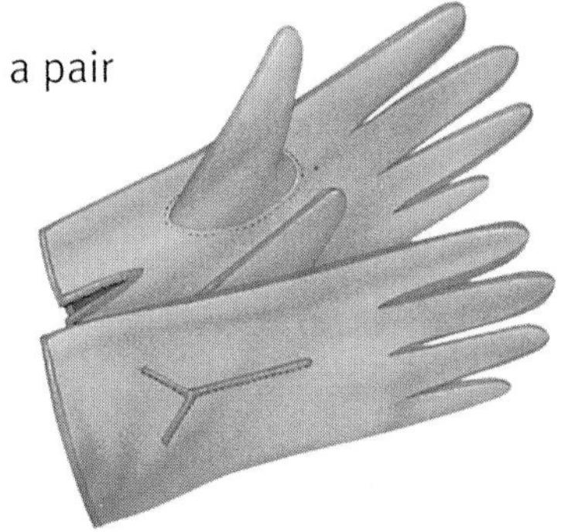
a pair

palace NOUN a large and magnificent house where an important person lives, usually a king or queen.

pale ADJECTIVE not having much colour.

palm NOUN **1** the inside of your hand between your wrist and your fingers. **2** a tall tree with no branches but a lot of leaves at the top.

pan NOUN a container with a handle that you use on a stove to cook food in.

pancake NOUN a thin, flat round of batter cooked in a frying-pan.

panda NOUN a large, bear-like animal which comes from China and has black and white fur.

panic NOUN a very strong feeling of fear that makes you lose control of your actions.

panic VERB (panicking, panicked) to have such a feeling.

pant VERB to breathe with short, quick gasps.

pantomime NOUN a funny, musical entertainment for children performed at Christmas.

paper NOUN **1** sheets of material for writing or printing on, or for covering things. **2** a newspaper.

parachute NOUN a device made mostly of a large piece of material that you strap to your body so you can drop safely from an aeroplane.

parachute

parcel NOUN something wrapped up in paper.

parent NOUN a mother or father. *He lives with his parents.*

park NOUN a large, public area of grass and trees, usually in a town.

park VERB to drive a vehicle into a position where you are going to leave it for a time.

parrot NOUN a bird with brightly coloured feathers that is often kept as a pet.

part NOUN **1** one of the pieces that something else is made up of. **2** a share in something. *He took no part in the robbery.* **3** the role that an actor has in a play, film, etc.

party NOUN (PLURAL parties) **1** a gathering of people to celebrate an event. **2** a group of people with the same political views.

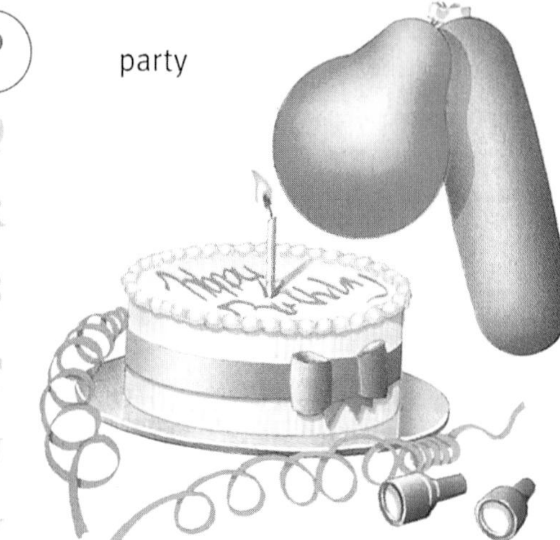

party

pass VERB **1** to go beyond or past. *We passed the station on our left.* **2** to give. *Please pass me the salt.* **3** to succeed in doing something. *Pass the exam.* **4** to go by. *Time passed.*

passenger NOUN someone who travels in a vehicle that is driven by someone else.

past 1 after. *Half past three.* **2** up to and then beyond. *The house is just past the golf course.*

past ADJECTIVE belonging to the past.

past NOUN the time before the present.

pasta

pasta NOUN food that is made from flour, eggs and water and comes in lots of different shapes. *Pasta shells.*

paste NOUN **1** a thin, wet glue for sticking paper. **2** a soft mixture of food, often spread on sandwiches.

pastry NOUN a dough-like mixture of flour and fat used for baking pies, flans, etc.

pat VERB (patting, patted) to tap lightly and repeatedly with the palm of your hand. *John patted the dog.*

did you know?

past

The spellings *passed* and *past* are sometimes confused. *Passed* comes from the verb *pass. We passed the garage. Time has passed by. Past* is used for all other forms. *The house is just past the golf course. Half past three. They are living in the past* (noun).

patch NOUN (PLURAL patches) **1** a piece of material that you use to cover a hole in something. *Mum sewed a patch over the hole in my jeans.* **2** a small piece of ground. *A vegetable patch.*

path NOUN a track you can walk or ride along. *A cycle path.*

patient ADJECTIVE able to stay calm and wait for something without getting cross.

patient NOUN a sick person who is being treated by a doctor or a nurse.

pattern NOUN **1** a regular design or arrangement of colours and shapes. **2** something you use as a guide or copy when making something. *A sewing pattern.*

pattern

pause NOUN *a* short stop.

pause VERB (pausing, paused) to stop for a short time.

pavement NOUN the path for you to walk on beside a road.

paw NOUN an animal's foot that has claws.

pay VERB (paid) to give money to buy something or in return for work done.

pea NOUN a small, round, green seed in a pod that is eaten as a vegetable.

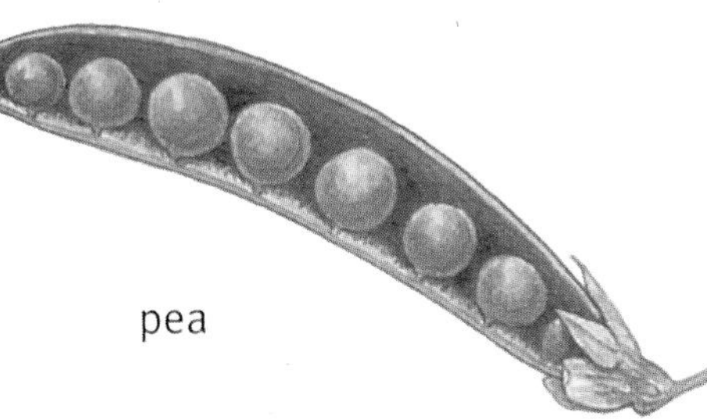

pea

peace NOUN **1** a time when there is no war or fighting between people. **2** calmness and quietness, rest.

peach NOUN (PLURAL peaches) a juicy, round fruit with a large stone in the middle.

peacock NOUN the male of a bird with long blue and green tail feathers that it can spread out like a fan.

peanut NOUN small, oval nut that is often eaten roasted or salted as a snack.

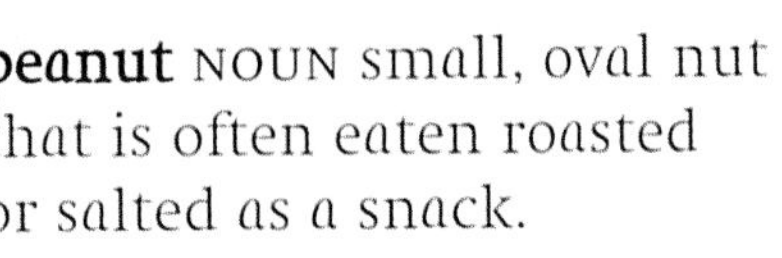

pear NOUN a sweet, juicy fruit which is wider at the bottom and narrower at the stalk.

pebble NOUN a small, smooth, round stone.

pedal NOUN the part of a machine that you push down on with your foot.

pedal VERB (pedalling, pedalled) to push a pedal down to make a bicycle, etc., move.

peel VERB to remove the skin from a fruit or vegetable.

pen NOUN an instrument you use with ink to write or draw.

pencil NOUN an instrument with a thin stick of lead through the middle that you write or draw with.

penguin NOUN a black and white Antarctic bird that cannot fly.

penny NOUN (PLURAL pennies or pence) a small coin, a hundredth part of £1.

people *See* **person**.

pepper NOUN **1** a powdered spice used to flavour food. **2** a red or green vegetable that can be eaten raw or cooked.

person NOUN (PLURAL people) a man, woman, or child, a human being.

peel

persuade VERB (persuading, persuaded) to influence someone to do or believe something. *Persuade me to stay.*

peacock

did you know?

penguin

People who study the history and origin of words have puzzled for a long time over the origin of the word *penguin*. The best guess is that it comes from the Welsh *pen* 'head' and *gwyn* 'white', perhaps originally referring to the now extinct bird, the auk.

A B C D E F G H I J K L M N O P Q R S T U V W X Y Z

pet NOUN an animal that you keep for company and enjoyment. *Pet rabbit.*

petal NOUN one of the coloured parts that make up a flower head.

petal

petrol NOUN the fuel used in car engines.

photograph NOUN a picture taken on film with a camera and then developed.

piano NOUN a large, musical instrument with black and white keys which you press to make different notes.

pick VERB **1** to choose. *Pick a card.* **2** to remove something with your fingers. *Pick your nose.* **3** to collect. *Pick flowers.*

picnic NOUN a meal that you eat outdoors.

picture NOUN a painting, drawing or photograph.

pie NOUN meat, vegetables or fruit baked in pastry.

did you know?

pilgrim

In the Middle Ages Christian pilgrims journeyed to visit holy places and shrines.

They sometimes travelled as far as Jerusalem.

It was about such pilgrims that Chaucer wrote his famous book 'The Canterbury Tales'.

piece NOUN **1** a part of something. *A piece of cake.* **2** a single thing. *A piece of work.*

pig NOUN an animal kept on farms for its meat.

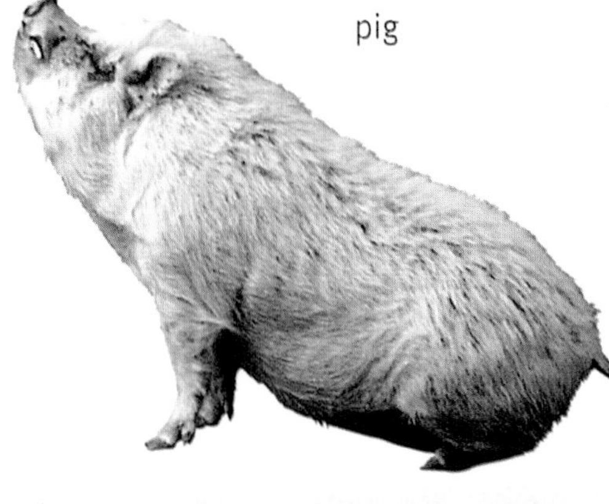

pig

picnic

pile NOUN a heap of things one on top of the other.

pilgrim NOUN somebody who travels to a holy place for religious reasons.

pill NOUN a small tablet of medicine that you swallow.

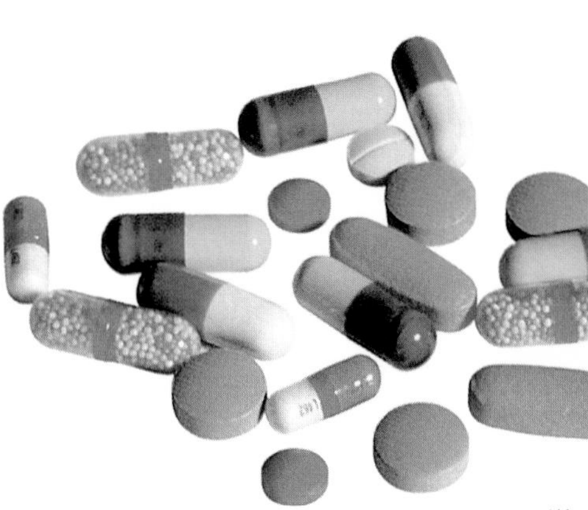

pill

pillow NOUN a cushion to rest your head on in bed.

pilot NOUN the person who flies an aeroplane or who guides a ship into a harbour.

pin NOUN a short, thin, pointed piece of metal that you stick through things to fasten them together.

pink ADJECTIVE pale red in colour.

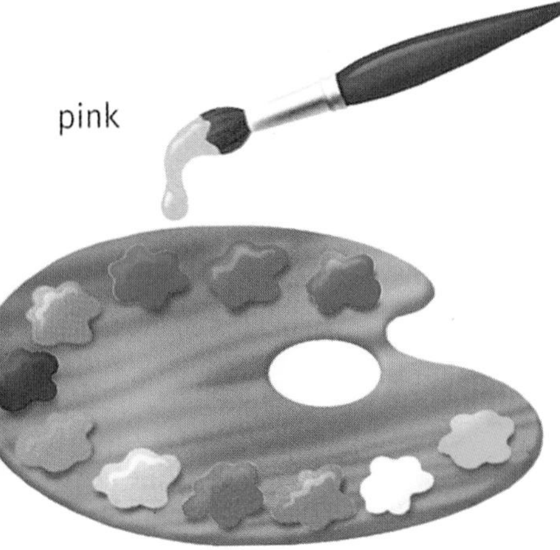
pink

plan VERB (planning, planned) to decide or intend to do something.

plane *See* **aeroplane**.

planet NOUN a large body in space that goes round the Sun. Earth, Mars and Saturn are planets.

plant NOUN any living thing that grows in the ground and has roots, a stem and leaves.

plant VERB to put a seed, etc., into the ground.

plastic NOUN a man-made material that is light and strong and has many uses.

play VERB **1** to have fun. **2** to take part in a game. **3** to perform a part in a play or film. **4** to make music on an instrument.

plastic

pipe NOUN **1** a long tube through which liquid or gas flows. **2** something used for smoking tobacco.

pirate NOUN someone who robs ships at sea.

pizza NOUN a flat, round piece of dough covered with tomatoes, cheese, etc., and baked in an oven.

pizza

place NOUN **1** any particular position or area. **2** a position in a competition or race. *We finished in second place.* **3** a seat. *Is this place free?*

plain ADJECTIVE **1** easy to understand or see. **2** not fancy, not decorated, simple.

plan NOUN **1** an arrangement that you make or an idea that you have in advance of doing something. **2** a drawing showing layouts, sizes etc.

plate NOUN a flat dish that you eat your food from.

platypus NOUN (PLURAL platypuses) an Australian animal with a beak like a duck.

play NOUN a story performed by actors in a theatre or on television.

playground NOUN an area where children can run about and have fun on slides, swings, etc.

playschool NOUN a nursery school or playgroup for children who are too young for junior school.

did you know?

planets

The planets in our solar system, in the order from nearest to farthest from the Sun, are:

Mercury, Venus, Earth, Mars, Jupiter, Saturn, Uranus, Neptune, Pluto.

When the sky is clear you can sometimes see Venus, which looks like a very bright star.

A B C D E F G H I J K L M N O P Q R S T U V W X Y Z

please VERB (pleasing, pleased) to make someone happy. *It pleased me when she asked me to go to her party.*

please said when you want to ask for something politely.

plenty an amount that is more than you need, enough. *I have plenty of money.*

plimsoll NOUN a light, sports shoe with a rubber sole.

plough NOUN a machine that farmers use to turn over and break up the soil.

plug NOUN **1** a device connected to an appliance that you put into an electrical socket. **2** something to block a hole, especially the device that you use to stop the water running out of a bath, washbasin or sink.

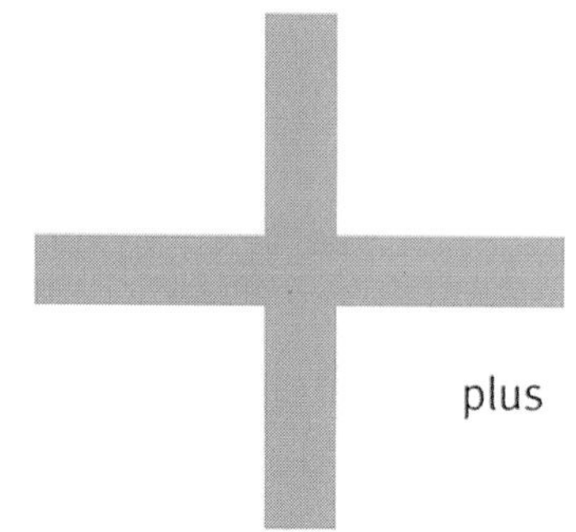
plus

plus with the addition of, and, the sign +.

pocket NOUN a small bag sewn into a piece of clothing for you to carry things in.

poem NOUN a piece of writing with the words arranged in short lines which often rhyme.

poet NOUN someone who writes poems.

point NOUN **1** the sharp end of something. **2** the main idea or purpose of something. **3** a mark or position on a compass, dial, etc. **4** a unit used to work out the score in a game, quiz, etc.

point VERB to use your finger to show the direction of something.

poison NOUN substance that could kill you if it gets into your body.

pole NOUN **1** a long, round stick or post. **2** one of the two points at either end of the earth. *The North and South Poles.* **3** one of the two ends of a magnet.

police PLURAL NOUN the men and women whose job is to make sure that people obey the law.

polite ADJECTIVE well-mannered. *A polite child.*

pond NOUN an area of water, smaller than a lake.

did you know?

plural

- The *plural* is the form of a word that you use when you want to talk about two or more people or things.

  For example, the plural of '*dog*' is '*dogs*'.
- The most common way to make a word into the plural is to add '*-s*': *book – books*.
- Some words add '*-es*', such as *church – churches*, *tomato – tomatoes*.
- Some words have irregular plurals: *child – children*, *foot – feet*, *goose – geese*.
- Where the plural is irregular, it is shown in this dictionary.

  See also ***singular***.

pony NOUN (PLURAL ponies) a small horse.

pool NOUN **1** a small area of water or a puddle. **2** a swimming pool.

pool

poor ADJECTIVE **1** owning very little or having very little money. **2** not of a good quality or amount.

pop NOUN **1** a sudden, sharp sound like that made when you pull a cork out of a bottle. **2** fizzy drink. **3** popular music.

pop VERB (popping, popped) to make a sudden, sound.

pop music NOUN modern music with a strong rhythm.

poppy NOUN (PLURAL poppies) wild plant with a red flower.

porridge NOUN soft food made from oats cooked in water and milk.

port NOUN a harbour or a town which has a harbour.

possible ADJECTIVE able to happen or to be done.

post NOUN **1** the way that letters and parcels are collected, sorted and delivered. **2** an upright piece of wood, metal or concrete fixed into the ground.

post VERB to send a letter or parcel through the post.

pot NOUN a round container for cooking and keeping things in.

pottery NOUN pots, plates and other objects that are made from clay and then baked hard in an oven.

potato NOUN (PLURAL potatoes) a white vegetable with a brown or red skin that grows under the ground and can be cooked and served in many ways.

pour VERB **1** to make a liquid flow. **2** to rain heavily. *It poured with rain.*

poppies

porcupine NOUN a small animal with long prickles over its back and sides.

pork NOUN meat that comes from a pig.

porcupine

postcard NOUN a card for sending a message through the postal system without an envelope.

postcode NOUN a group of letters and figures added to an address to help the post office sort mail.

Post Office NOUN the national organization in charge of postal services.

post office a building or a place in a building where you can buy stamps and send letters.

did you know?

prefix

- A *prefix* is a group of letters that you add to the beginning of a word to make a new word.

  For example 'un' is added to *happy* to make *unhappy*, meaning 'not happy'.

  Other examples: 'bi-', meaning 'two' (a *biplane* has two wings), 'extra-' meaning 'outside', 'beyond' for example, *'extraterrestrial'* means from beyond earth.

  See also ***suffix***.

preposition

- A *preposition* is a word such as *at*, *by*, *for* or *with*.
- Prepositions often show the position or location of something.
- They are usually put in front of a noun.

  For example, in '*under the table*' '*under*' is a preposition.

powder

powder NOUN anything that has been crushed or ground into tiny particles.

power NOUN **1** the strength or ability to do something. **2** the legal right to do something. **3** a person or group with a lot of control over other people.

practice NOUN an action that you do regularly.

practise VERB (practising, practised) to keep doing something over and over again to get better at it.

prawn NOUN a shellfish similar to a shrimp.

pretty

prepare VERB (preparing, prepared) to get something ready or to make yourself ready for something. *I always prepare for school by making sure that my homework is complete.*

present NOUN **1** a gift. **2** the time that is now here.

present ADJECTIVE **1** in the place spoken of. *Were you present at the prize-giving?* **2** happening or existing now. *The present owner.*

president NOUN the head of government in countries like the United States of America.

press VERB **1** to push firmly. *I pressed the doorbell with my finger.* **2** to make flat or smooth. *We press flowers to make them flat. They can then be placed inside books.*

pretend VERB to act as though things are not as they really are. *I like to pretend that I am a famous person.*

pretty ADJECTIVE (prettier, prettiest) very nice to look at. *The shell is very pretty.*

price NOUN the amount of money something costs. *I asked the salesperson what the price of the coat was.*

priceless ADJECTIVE worth a lot of money, very valuable. *The painting in the gallery was priceless.*

priest NOUN a religious leader. *A Catholic priest.*

prim ADJECTIVE very correct and easily shocked by anything rude. *She is very prim. She will never laugh at rude jokes.*

primary colour NOUN red, yellow or blue. All other colours can made by mixing these three colours in different ways.

primary school NOUN a school for children usually between 5 and 11 years old.

prime minister NOUN the head of government in countries like the United Kingdom.

primrose NOUN a wild plant that has pale yellow flowers.

did you know?

pronoun

- A *pronoun* is a word that is used instead of a noun.

  For example in the sentence: *Colin came home and then he played on the computer*, 'he' is a pronoun.

  The word 'he' is used to avoid repeating the noun 'Colin'.

princess NOUN (PLURAL princesses) **1** the daughter of a king or queen. **2** the wife of a prince.

princess

print VERB **1** to put words and pictures onto paper using a machine. **2** to write without using joined-up letters.

printer NOUN **1** someone whose job is printing. **2** a machine that prints out information from a computer.

prison NOUN a building in which criminals are locked up.

prize NOUN something awarded for good work or for winning a competition or game.

problem NOUN a difficulty, a question that needs answering. *Problem solving.*

program NOUN a set of computer instructions.

did you know?

proverb

- A *proverb* is a short sentence that gives advice or makes a comment about life.

  Examples of proverbs are:

  A bird in the hand is worth two in the bush.

  Beggars cannot be choosers.

  More haste, less speed.

  Too many cooks spoil the broth.

programme NOUN **1** a play, show, item, etc., on the radio or television. **2** a leaflet giving details of events that are going to take place in a sporting fixture, during a performance, etc.

project NOUN a subject studied in detail.

promise VERB (promising, promised) to say that you will or will not do something. *I promised that I would take my brother to the sweet shop.*

pronounce VERB (pronouncing, pronounced) to say a word in the way that it is usually said or in a particular way.

protect VERB to guard someone or something from harm. *The guard dog protects the house.*

proud ADJECTIVE feeling that you are better than other people. *I was proud of myself when I won first prize in the school swimming competition.*

prove VERB (proving, proved) to show for certain that something is true. *I proved that I was telling the truth by showing them the letter.*

prowl VERB to move about quietly, trying not to be seen or heard. *The lion is prowling in search of food.*

prune NOUN a dried plum. *Prunes are very good for the digestion.*

prune VERB to cut off or shorten branches of a tree or bush. *I pruned the rose bush in the garden.*

pub NOUN a place where you can buy and drink alcohol. *My uncle owns a pub.*

pudding NOUN **1** a sweet food that is cooked and served hot. *Chocolate pudding.* **2** the dessert course of a meal. *What's for pudding?*

puffin NOUN seabird with a brightly coloured beak. *The puffin perched on the*

puffin

A B C D E F G H I J K L M N O **P** Q R S T U V W X Y Z

puddle NOUN a small pool of water, especially one left after it has been raining.

puddle

puff NOUN a small amount of air or smoke blown out of something.

pull VERB to drag something along behind you or move it towards you.

pulp NOUN **1** soft inner part of a fruit or vegetable. **2** a soft mass of other material.

pulpit NOUN a small platform for the preacher in a church.

pumpkins

pulse NOUN **1** the regular beating of blood as it is pumped through the body by the heart. *I can feel my pulse when I touch my wrists.* **2** the regular beat or throbbing of music.

puma NOUN a large wild cat of western America, also called a cougar or mountain lion.

pump NOUN a machine used to force a liquid or gas to flow in a certain direction.

pumpkin NOUN a large, round, deep yellow fruit.

punch VERB to hit with your fist.

puncture NOUN a small hole made by a sharp object, especially in a tyre.

puncture VERB to make or get a puncture. *A nail in the road must have punctured my tyre.*

punish VERB to make someone suffer for something that they have done wrong. *We were punished for making a mess.*

pupil NOUN **1** someone who is being taught. **2** the round, black part in the middle of your eye.

puppet

puppet NOUN **1** a toy figure that moves when you pull wires or strings. **2** a cloth figure that you put on your hand like a glove and move with your fingers.

puppy NOUN (PLURAL puppies) a young dog.

puppy

pure ADJECTIVE not mixed with anything else, clean. *The water from the spring was pure enough to drink.*

purple ADJECTIVE of a colour between red and blue.

purr VERB to make a low sound like a cat when it is pleased. *My cat always purrs loudly when I stroke him.*

purse NOUN a small bag for money.

push VERB to press hard against something to try to move it away from you. *I pushed the door hard until it opened.*

did you know?

punctuation

We use punctuation marks to make what we are writing easy to follow.

Examples of punctuation marks are: **apostrophe**, **brackets**, **colon**, **comma**, **exclamation mark**, **full stop**, **inverted commas**, **question mark** and **semi-colon**. If you want to find out more about them, look them up in this dictionary.

pushy ADJECTIVE unpleasantly keen to get things done so as to make yourself noticed. *Amanda is very pushy. She always puts her hand up first when the teacher asks a question.*

pussyfoot VERB to act very cautiously.

put VERB (putting, put) to place something in a particular position. *I put the cup down on the table.*

putty NOUN a soft paste used to fix glass into window frames or fill holes.

puzzle NOUN **1** a difficult problem or question, something that is hard to understand. **2** a game in which things have to be fitted together properly. *A crossword puzzle.*

pyjamas PLURAL NOUN a loose jacket and trousers that you wear in bed.

puzzle

pylon NOUN a tall metal structure used for holding wires that carry electricity over long distances.

pyramid NOUN **1** a shape with a flat base and three or four sloping sides that come to a point at the top. **2** an ancient stone building in the shape of a pyramid constructed over the tombs of the ancient kings and queens of Egypt.

did you know?

pyjamas

According to the history of the word, pyjamas are leg clothes. The word comes via India, from Persian *pai*, meaning 'foot' or 'leg' and *jamah*, meaning 'garment'. It was used to describe loose trousers, made of silk or cotton, which were worn in countries such as India, Turkey and Iran. Some of the Europeans living in these countries wore them, particularly to sleep in. They brought them back to Europe, where a pyjama jacket top was added for the upper part of the body, to keep the wearer warm in the cooler climate.

python NOUN a large snake that kills by winding its body round animals and squeezing them.

Qq

quack VERB to make a loud harsh noise like that of a duck.

quality NOUN (PLURAL qualities) **1** how good or bad something is. **2** something good in a person's character, what a person or thing is like.

quantity NOUN (PLURAL quantities) the amount of something.

quarrel NOUN an argument. *We had a quarrel.*

quarrel

quarry NOUN a place where people dig stone out of the ground to use for buildings and other things.

quarter NOUN **1** one of the four equal parts that something is divided into. *Kate ate a quarter of the cake.* **2** 15 minutes past or 15 minutes to the hour when telling the time. *At quarter past 11.*

queen

quay NOUN a platform for ships to dock at. *The ships docked at the quay.*

queen NOUN **1** the female ruler of a country. **2** the wife of a king. **3** a chess piece.

did you know?

question mark

- The sign (?) is called a *question mark.*
- It is put at the end of a sentence to show that it is a question.
- For example, '*What time is it?*' and '*Why are you late?*'

question NOUN something that you ask someone.

queue NOUN people or vehicles waiting in a line.

quiche NOUN a tart with a savoury filling.

quick ADJECTIVE fast, not slow.

quiet ADJECTIVE **1** making no noise. **2** still.

quilt NOUN a thick bed-cover.

quit VERB (quitting, quitted) to leave or stop doing something. *Don't forget to quit the computer program before you turn off the computer.*

quite 1 completely. *I'm not quite sure.* **2** rather. *They took quite a long time.*

quiz NOUN (PLURAL quizzes) a competition or game which tests your knowledge.

quotation NOUN a person's written or spoken words repeated exactly by somebody else.

quotation marks PLURAL NOUN the punctuation marks (' ') or (" ") used before and after words somebody has said.

quote VERB (quoting, quoted) to repeat the exact words that someone else has written or said.

quilt

Rr

radio

rabbit NOUN a small animal with long ears that lives in burrows or may be kept in a hutch as a pet.

rabbits

race NOUN a competition to see who is the fastest at something. *A cycle race.*

race VERB (racing, raced) to compete in a race.

racket NOUN **1** a light bat with strings across it for hitting the ball in sports such as tennis or squash. **2** a loud and terrible noise.

radiator NOUN **1** a device that heats a room when it is connected to a central heating system. **2** the part of a car engine that keeps it cool.

radio NOUN **1** sounds broadcast over the airwaves. **2** a device for receiving these sounds.

rag NOUN a torn piece of old cloth.

rail NOUN **1** a bar or rod. **2** one of the parallel steel bars that a train runs on.

railway NOUN **1** steel track on which trains run. **2** company that runs this system of tracks and trains.

rain NOUN drops of water that fall from clouds in the sky.

rainbow NOUN an arch of colours that you sometimes see in the sky after it has been raining.

raincoat NOUN a waterproof coat that you wear when it's raining.

raise VERB (raising, raised) to lift up. *I raised my hands in the air.*

ran *See* **run**. *I ran across the park.*

rang *See* **ring**. *The telephone rang.*

rare ADJECTIVE not common, unusual. *He was suffering from a rare disease.*

rat NOUN an animal with a long tail that looks like a mouse but is bigger.

rattle NOUN a baby's toy that makes a noise when you shake it.

raw ADJECTIVE not cooked. *The vegetables were raw.*

rat

A B C D E F G H I J K L M N O P Q R S T U V W X Y Z

reach

reach VERB **1** to stretch out your arm to touch something. **2** to arrive at.

read VERB to be able to understand words written or printed on a page.

ready ADJECTIVE (readier, readiest) **1** prepared. *Dinner's ready.* **2** willing. *Are you nearly ready to go?*

real ADJECTIVE **1** that actually exists and is not imagined. **2** genuine. *A real diamond.*

realize VERB (realizing, realized) to become aware of something.

really truthfully, in fact.

reason NOUN **1** an excuse, explanation or cause. **2** the ability to think or understand.

record NOUN **1** a written account of something that has been done or has happened. **2** a round piece of plastic onto which music has been recorded. **3** the very best ever achieved.

recorder NOUN a musical instrument which you blow into to play.

red ADJECTIVE (redder, reddest) having the colour of blood.

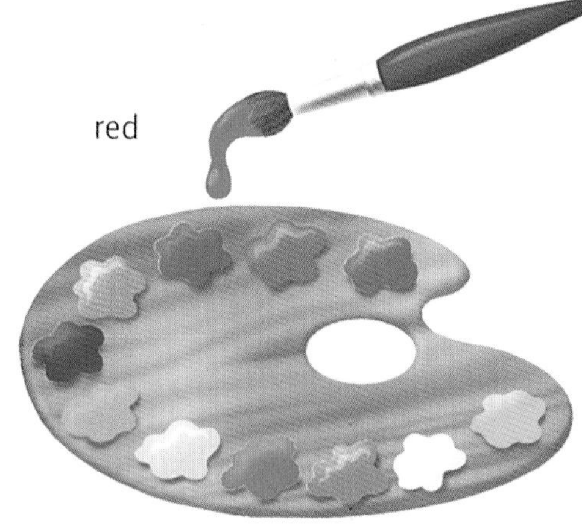

red

reflection NOUN an image that you see in a mirror or in water.

refrigerator NOUN a device for keeping food and drink cool.

refuse VERB (refusing, refused) to say 'no'.

register NOUN a list of names.

reindeer NOUN (PLURAL reindeer) a kind of deer that lives in cold places.

remember VERB to keep something in your mind, not to forget.

did you know?

remember

We can use an expression to help us to remember something else. For the order of the colours in the rainbow: **R**ichard **o**f **Y**ork **g**ave **b**attle **i**n **v**ain. (Red, Orange, Yellow, Green, Blue, Indigo, Violet.)

remind VERB to cause you to remember or think about something or someone.

repair VERB to mend.

repeat VERB to say, do or happen again.

reply VERB (replying, replied) to answer.

report NOUN an account of how well or badly a pupil has done at school.

report VERB to give an account of something that has happened.

rescue VERB (rescuing, rescued) to save someone from danger or captivity.

rescue

rest NOUN **1** a time of not doing anything tiring, sleep. **2** what remains or is left over.

rest VERB not to do anything active, to relax.

restaurant NOUN place where you can buy and eat meals.

result NOUN **1** the effect of certain actions or events. **2** the final score in a game, competition, etc.

return VERB **1** to come or go back. **2** to send or give back.

reward NOUN something that you get for doing something good or helpful.

rhinoceros NOUN (PLURAL rhinoceroses) a large animal with a thick skin and one or two horns on its nose.

rhinoceros

rhyme NOUN **1** a word ending with a similar sound as another. **2** a short poem. *Nursery rhyme.*

rhyme VERB (rhyming, rhymed) to have a similar sound.

ribbon NOUN a narrow length of material for tying or decorating things with. *The dress was covered in clusters of pink ribbons.*

rice NOUN a plant that grows in hot, wet places and produces white or brown grains that you cook and eat.

rice

rich ADJECTIVE **1** having a lot of money and goods, wealthy. **2** splendid and valuable. **3** full of goodness or colour.

ridden *See* **ride**. *Have you ever ridden a horse?*

riddle NOUN a puzzling question. *Ask me a riddle.*

ride VERB (riding, rode, ridden) **1** to travel in a vehicle. **2** to travel on a horse or a bicycle.

right 1 on the right. *The right-hand side.* **2** straight. *Right on at the lights.* **3** exactly. *Right on time.*

right ADJECTIVE **1** correct. *Did you get the right answer?* **2** good.

ribbon

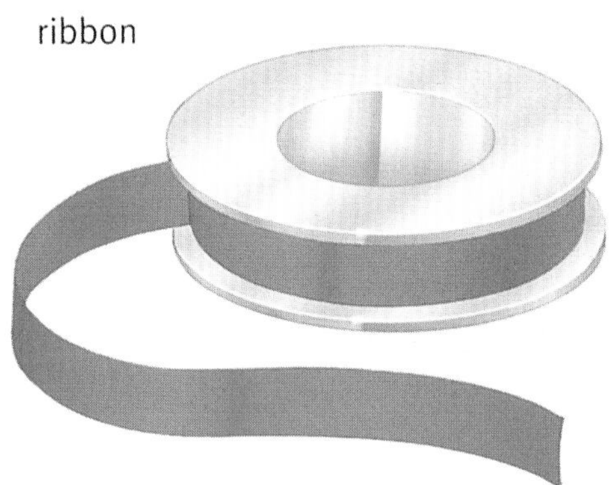

ring NOUN **1** a circle or something in the shape of a circle. **2** a piece of jewellery to wear on your finger. **3** a closed-in space with seats round it where a contest or performance takes place.

ring VERB (rang, rung) **1** to sound a bell. **2** to make a sound like a bell. **3** to make a telephone call.

rinse VERB (rinsing, rinsed) to wash in water without soap.

ripe ADJECTIVE ready to eat.

ripe

rise VERB (rising, rose, risen) **1** to get up. **2** to move upwards. *Steam rising.*

risen *See* **rise**. *They had risen early.*

river NOUN wide stream of water flowing across land to the sea.

road NOUN track with a hard surface on which vehicles travel.

did you know?

river

The longest river in the world is in Africa. The river Nile starts at Burundi in central Africa, and flows for 6690 km before reaching the Mediterranean Sea on the coast of Egypt.

roar VERB to make a sound like a lion.

roast VERB to cook food in an oven or over an open fire.

rob VERB (robbing, robbed) to steal money or property from someone.

robin NOUN a small garden bird with a red breast.

robot NOUN a machine made to act like a person.

rock NOUN **1** the hard stone that the earth is made of. **2** a large piece of stone. **3** a hard sweet in the shape of a stick.

rocket NOUN **1** a space vehicle or missile. **2** a firework.

rocket

rod NOUN a long, straight stick or bar.

rode *See* **ride**. *She rode the bicycle along the street.*

roll NOUN **1** a long piece of something wound around itself into a tube shape. **2** a small loaf of bread for one person.

did you know?

rock

There are three types of rock: metamorphic, sedimentary and igneous. They are each formed in different ways from minerals and animal remains. The Earth is covered by a crust of solid rock.

roll VERB **1** to turn over and over, like a ball. **2** to make something into a round shape. **3** to make something flat and smooth by passing a rounded object over it.

roller skates PLURAL NOUN wheels fitted to the soles of shoes for skating over flat surfaces.

roof NOUN the outside covering of the top part of a building, vehicle, etc.

room NOUN **1** one of the areas into which a building is divided, with its own walls, ceiling and floor. **2** enough space for something.

root NOUN the part of a plant that grows underground.

rope NOUN strong, thick cord made of separate threads twisted together.

round

rose NOUN a beautiful flower that grows on a stem with thorns.

rose *See* **rise**. *The sun rose.*

rose

rotten ADJECTIVE gone bad and not fit to eat or use. *The apple was too rotten to eat.*

rough ADJECTIVE **1** not smooth or even. *A rough edge.* **2** stormy. *A rough sea.* **3** done quickly, not accurate. *A rough drawing.*

round 1 spinning or moving in circles. *The wheels went round.* **2** surrounding. *The path goes round the lake.* **3** in or into all parts. *They showed us round the house.*

round ADJECTIVE shaped like a ball.

round NOUN **1** one stage in a competition or sporting event. **2** one of a series of regular visits that people make during their work. *A paper round.* **3** a whole slice of bread.

roundabout NOUN **1** a place where several roads meet and cars drive in a circle. **2** a merry-go-round.

rounders NOUN a team game played with a bat and ball.

route NOUN the way you take to get to a place. *I took my usual route to work.*

routine ADJECTIVE with little variety. *I have a routine job.*

routine NOUN the usual way of doing things. *Getting up late upsets my routine.*

row (said like **no**) NOUN people or things in a neat and tidy line.

row VERB to move a boat through water using oars. *I rowed the boat along the river*

row (said like **how**) NOUN **1** an argument, a quarrel. **2** a loud noise.

royal ADJECTIVE belonging to or connected with a king or queen.

rub VERB (rubbing, rubbed) to move something backwards and forwards against something else. *I used a tissue to rub the mark off my jacket.*

royal

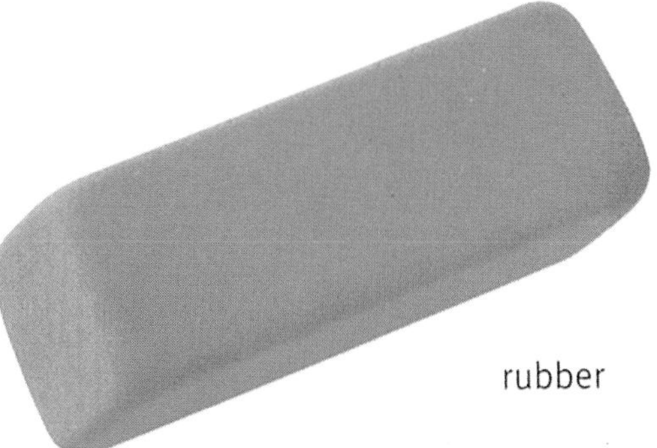
rubber

rubber NOUN **1** the strong, elastic material from which Wellingtons, tyres etc., are made. **2** a piece of this used to remove pencil marks.

rubbish NOUN **1** waste material. *A pile of rubbish.* **2** silly nonsense. *Everything he said was a load of rubbish!*

rude ADJECTIVE **1** not polite. *He was very rude to me.* **2** not decent. A rude joke. *The joke that she told was very rude.*

rug NOUN **1** a mat for the floor. **2** a thick blanket.

rugby NOUN a team game played with an oval ball.

ruin VERB to completely spoil or damage something. *The stain on my dress has completely ruined it.*

rule VERB (ruling, ruled) **1** to govern. *The king ruled wisely throughout his reign.* **2** to make a decision. *The ball was ruled out of play.* **3** to draw a straight line.

ruler NOUN **1** someone who governs a country. *He was the ruler of the kingdom.* **2** a long, straight-edged piece of wood, plastic, etc., used to draw straight lines or to measure things with.

did you know?

rubber

Natural rubber is made from latex, which comes from trees grown in tropical countries. The latex is tapped from the trees through holes made in the bark. We can also make rubber from chemicals.

run VERB (running, ran, run) **1** to move on your legs at the fastest pace. **2** to work. *The car costs a lot to run.* **3** to flow or drip down. *The paint ran.* **4** to go or continue. *The motorway runs for miles.* **5** to be in charge of something. *He runs his father's business.*

rung NOUN a bar in a ladder. *My foot was on the bottom rung when I fell off the ladder and broke my arm.*

rung *See* **ring**. *Have you rung the bell?*

runner NOUN **1** a person who runs, especially in a race. **2** a thin wooden or metal strip on which something slides or moves.

rush VERB to hurry.

rust NOUN the brown substance that forms on iron that has come into contact with water.

rust

Ss

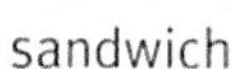
sandwich

sack NOUN **1** a large bag made out of a rough material. **2** the loss of your job. *My boss said my work was poor, so I got the sack.*

sad ADJECTIVE (sadder, saddest) feeling unhappy.

safe ADJECTIVE not in danger.

safe NOUN a strong locked box for keeping valuable things secure.

said *See* **say**. *I said 'Go.'*

sail NOUN piece of cloth fixed to the mast of a boat so that it catches the wind and moves the boat through the water.

sail VERB **1** to travel on water. **2** to control a boat on water.

sail

sailor NOUN someone who works on a boat as a member of the crew.

salad NOUN raw vegetables or fruit mixed together and eaten with other foods as part of a meal.

salt NOUN tiny, white grains that you put on your food to flavour it.

did you know?

sandwich

The name of this snack comes from the 18th-century John Montagu, 4th Earl of Sandwich. He was very fond of gambling and it is said that some of his games lasted as long as two days non-stop. Rather than interrupt the game and leave the table to eat food, he ordered his servant to bring him two slices of bread with layers of cold beef between them – and so this convenient snack came to be associated with his name.

same 1 exactly like something else. *The twins wore the same clothes.* **2** not changed. *She was just the same as I remembered her.* **3** always only one thing or person. *We go to the same school.*

sand NOUN tiny grains of stone, such as you find on the beach or in the desert.

sandals PLURAL NOUN open shoes for wearing in the summer, with straps that go over the top of your feet.

sandwich NOUN two slices of bread with a filling in between them.

sang *See* **sing**. *We sang carols.*

sank *See* **sink**. *The ship sank.*

sat *See* **sit**. *The children sat still.*

satchel NOUN a bag with a shoulder strap that you carry your school books in.

satellite NOUN **1** a man-made device sent into space to collect signals which it sends back to earth.

satellite dish NOUN large round metal object fixed to buildings to collect television signals which are sent using satellites in space.

satellite

did you know?

scissors

The word scissors is a plural noun – the same form of the word is used for the singular and plural. We do not say *one scissor*. Other plural nouns include: *binoculars*, *dregs*, *jeans*, *remains*, *sunglasses* and *trousers*.

Saturday NOUN the day of the week that comes after Friday and before Sunday.

sauce NOUN a thick liquid that you put on your food to flavour it.

saucepan NOUN a pan with a lid and a handle, that you use to cook food in.

saucepan

saucer NOUN a small dish on which you put a cup.

sausage NOUN a thin tube of skin filled with a mixture of meat, cereal, spices, etc.

save VERB (saving, saved) **1** to rescue from danger. **2** to keep something so that you can use it later. **3** to stop wasting something. **4** to stop a ball from going into a goal.

saw NOUN a tool with a zigzag blade that you use to cut things like wood.

saw *See* **see**. *Laura saw her sister coming towards her.*

saw

say VERB (said) **1** to speak. **2** to give your opinion.

scales PLURAL NOUN a weighing machine.

scare VERB (scaring, scared) to frighten.

scarf NOUN (PLURAL scarves or scarfs) a length of cloth you wear round your neck, usually to keep warm.

school NOUN a place where children go to learn.

science NOUN the study of how natural things behave and the knowledge that we have about them.

science

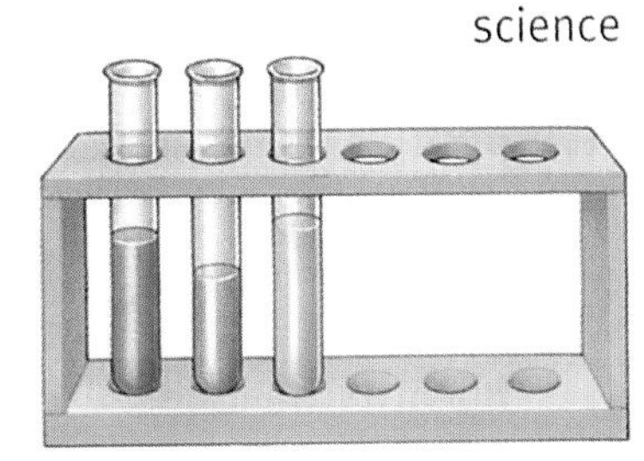

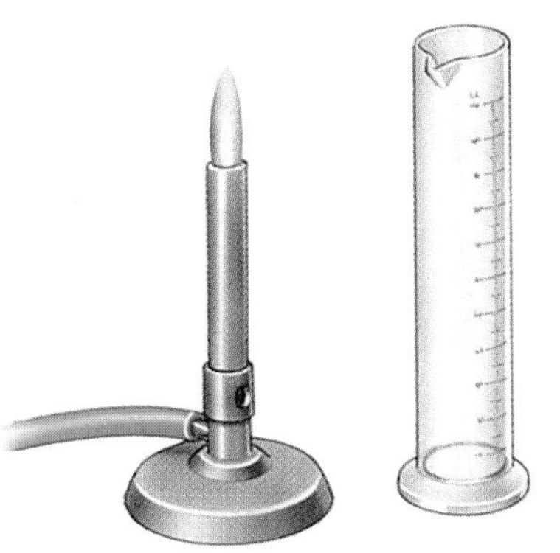

scissors PLURAL NOUN a pair of hinged blades that you use to cut things with.

scissors

scooter NOUN **1** a child's toy with a handle, two wheels and a platform for the feet. **2** a kind of motorcycle.

score NOUN the number of points, goals, etc., made in a game. *The score showed that we were going to win the match.*

scratch NOUN a mark or wound made by scratching.

scratch VERB **1** to damage a surface with something sharp and rough. *Our cat is always scratching furniture with his claws.* **2** to rub your skin to stop it itching. *Jamie scratched his arm.*

scream VERB to give a loud, high-pitched cry. *We all screamed with excitement on the rollercoaster ride.*

screen NOUN **1** a flat surface on which films are shown. **2** the front surface of a television, computer monitor, etc. **3** a frame which protects people from heat and cold or hides something from view.

screw NOUN piece of metal like a nail but with a thread around it. It is put into hard surfaces with a screwdriver.

screwdriver NOUN a tool used for turning screws.

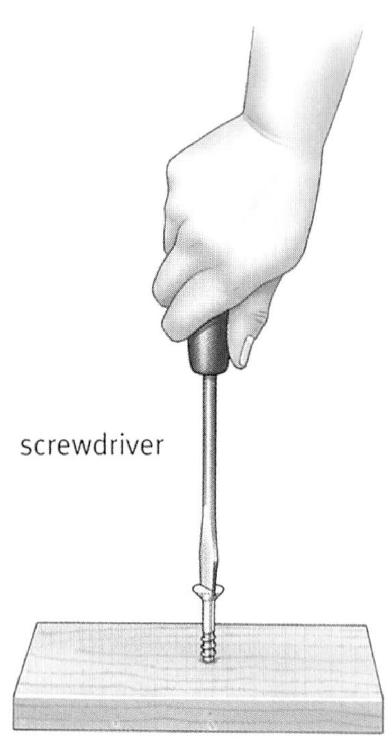
screwdriver

sea NOUN the salt water that covers most of the earth's surface. *A calm sea.*

seal NOUN **1** a sea creature that eats fish and swims by using flippers. **2** a mark, often made from wax, that is fixed to important things to show that they are genuine.

seal VERB **1** to put a seal on something. **2** to fasten something firmly. **3** to make something airtight.

search VERB to look for, to try to find. *Search party.*

seaside NOUN the place next to the sea, especially where people go for their holidays.

season NOUN **1** one of the four parts into which the year is divided: spring, summer, autumn and winter. **2** a time in the year for a particular activity. *The football season.*

seat NOUN something on which you sit.

second ADJECTIVE being the one after the first, 2nd.

second NOUN **1** a length of time. *There are 60 seconds in one minute.* **2** a brief moment.

secret NOUN something that only a few people know.

see VERB (saw, seen) **1** to look at something through your eyes. *I could see the hills in the distance.* **2** to understand. *I see what you mean.* **3** to meet or visit. *I went to see my friend.*

seed NOUN the part of a plant from which a new one grows.

seed

did you know?

sentence

- A *sentence* is a group of words starting with a capital letter and ending with a full stop, question mark or exclamation mark.
- The following are all examples of sentences.

  I like sweets.
  Where is your school?
  Go away!
- Most sentences have a verb.

  Below is an example of two sentences without verbs:

  'Yes.'
  'For heaven's sake!'

seem VERB to appear to be.

seen *See* **see**. *Have you seen this video?*

seesaw NOUN a plank, balanced so that when children sit on either end, one end goes up as the other comes down.

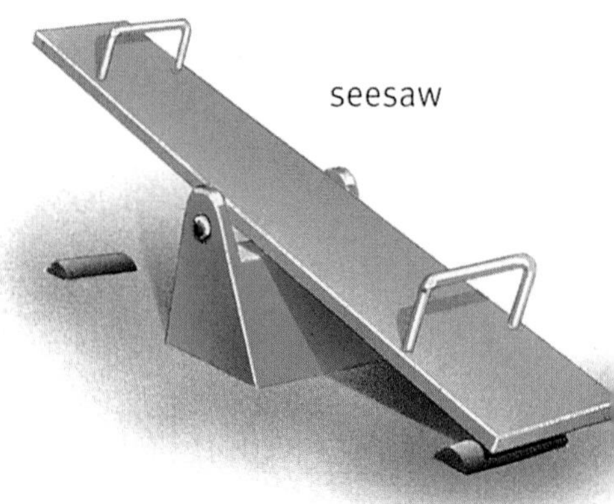
seesaw

selfish ADJECTIVE not caring about others, thinking only of yourself.

sell VERB (sold) to part with things in return for money. *She sold her house.*

Sellotape NOUN (trademark) sticky tape on a roll.

semi-circle NOUN a half circle. *We stood in a semi-circle.*

semi-colon NOUN The punctuation mark (;) is called *a semi-colon*. It is used to join two parts of a sentence and is used instead of 'and', 'but' or another conjunction. For example, in the sentence, *'I am very tired; I am also hungry.'* the semi-colon is used instead of *'and'*.

send VERB (sent) to cause or order someone or something to go or be taken somewhere. *James was sent to the headteacher's office.*

sensible ADJECTIVE having the ability to make good decisions.

sent *See* **send**. *I've sent her a birthday card.*

September NOUN the ninth month of the year, after August and before October.

September

set NOUN a collection of things. *A set of encyclopedias.*

set VERB (setting, set) **1** to put into a position. **2** to give someone work to do. *What homework has been set?* **3** to become hard. *The concrete set quickly in the warm sun.* **4** to go down below the horizon. *The sun sets earlier in the winter.* **5** to prepare a table for a meal.

7 seven

seven the number 7.

seventeen the number 17.

seventy the number 70.

sew VERB (sewed, sewn or sewed) to stitch material together with a needle and thread. *Sew a dress.*

sewn *See* **sew**. *I've sewn on a new button.*

shade NOUN **1** area sheltered from the sun or strong light. *Stand in the shade.* **2** something that keeps out light or makes it less bright. *A lampshade.* **3** a slightly different depth of colour. *A lighter shade of blue.*

shadow NOUN **1** an area of shade. **2** the dark shape cast by an object where it blocks out the light.

shake VERB (shaking, shook, shaken) **1** to move something up and down and from side to side very quickly. **2** to take someone by the right hand as a sign of greeting or agreement. **3** to shiver.

shaken *See* **shake**. *After you've shaken the bottle, pour the milk.*

shall to intend to happen, to happen in the future. *I shall be on holiday next week.*

did you know?

seven

The Seven Wonders of the World were seven outstanding man-made objects that were built in ancient times. Only one of these ancient wonders, the Pyramids, exists today.

There are still about eighty Pyramids in Egypt. The Great Pyramid at Giza is 137 m high. It would have taken thousands of slaves to build it.

shallow ADJECTIVE not deep.

shampoo NOUN special soap to wash your hair with.

shampoo

shan't = shall not. *We shan't be coming to the party.*

shape NOUN the form that something has, an outline.

shapes

share NOUN a part or portion of something. *There were many guests at the birthday party, but we all had a share of the cake.*

share VERB (sharing, shared) **1** to use or do something with others. *The friends shared a flat.* **2** to divide. *She shared her sandwiches with her friend.*

A B C D E F G H I J K L M N O P Q R S T U V W X Y Z

shark NOUN a dangerous fish with sharp teeth.

shark

sharp ADJECTIVE **1** having a fine point or a thin cutting edge. **2** thinking quickly.

shave VERB (shaving, shaved) to make your skin smooth by cutting off the hairs with a razor.

she (her, herself) that woman, girl or female animal.

she'd = she had, she would. *She'd have come if she could.*

she'll = she will. *She'll be here soon.*

she's = she is, she has. *She's a very nice girl.*

shed NOUN a small, wooden building for storing things in.

sheep NOUN (PLURAL sheep) a farm animal kept for its wool and meat.

sheep

sheet NOUN **1** large piece of cloth for covering a bed. **2** a single piece of paper.

shelf NOUN (PLURAL shelves) a length of board fixed to a wall or fitted in a cupboard on which you put things.

shell NOUN the hard, outside part of an egg, nut, snail, etc.

shelves *See* **shelf**.

shine VERB (shining, shone or shined) to give a bright light.

shiny ADJECTIVE (shinier, shiniest) giving a bright light.

ship NOUN a large boat.

shirt NOUN a piece of light clothing worn on the upper part of the body that has sleeves and a collar. *A red cotton shirt.*

shiver VERB to shake, often from fear or the cold.

shoe NOUN something that you wear over socks or tights to cover your foot.

shone *See* **shine**. *The sun shone brightly yesterday.*

shook *See* **shake**. *The wind shook the windows.*

shoot VERB (shot) **1** to fire a weapon at and hit a target. **2** to kick or throw a ball to score in a game. **3** to take a photograph or make a film.

shop NOUN somewhere goods are sold.

shore NOUN the land by the edge of the sea or a lake.

short ADJECTIVE **1** not long. *A short distance.* **2** not tall. *A short man.* **3** lasting only a little time. *A short break.*

shorts PLURAL NOUN short trousers. *Running shorts.*

shot *See* **shoot**. *The president was shot.*

should ought to. *You should be more polite.*

shoulder NOUN the part of your body at either side of your neck where your arms join it.

shells

shouldn't = should not. *You shouldn't have been so naughty.*

shout VERB to call out loudly. *The player shouted at the referee.*

show NOUN **1** a performance or entertainment. **2** a collection of things for people to look at. *A fine show of roses.*

show VERB (showed, shown) **1** to cause something to be seen. **2** to go with to guide. *Show me the way.* **3** to explain. *I'll show you how to do it.*

shower NOUN **1** a brief fall of rain. **2** a water-spraying device that you stand under to wash your body.

shower

shown *See* **show**. *I was shown how to work out the sums.*

shrank *See* **shrink**. *The clothes shrank in the rain.*

shout

shrimp NOUN a small sea creature.

shrink VERB (shrank, shrunk) to get smaller.

shrunk *See* **shrink**. *My favourite jumper has shrunk in the washing machine.*

shut VERB (shutting, shut) to close.

shy ADJECTIVE nervous and uncomfortable in the company of others.

sick ADJECTIVE poorly, not well.

did you know?

singular

- The *singular* is the form of a word that you use when you want to talk about one person or thing.
- This is in contrast to *plural*, which refers to two or more:

  '*book*' is singular;
  '*books*' is plural;
  '*child*' is singular;
  '*children*' is plural.

side NOUN **1** one of the flat surfaces of something such as a box. **2** not the front or the back. **3** a sports team.

sight NOUN **1** the ability to see. **2** something that is seen. **3** a place or view that is worth seeing, especially for tourists.

sign NOUN **1** an object or symbol that conveys a meaning. **2** a notice, giving information, directions, etc. *Follow the signs.*

silence NOUN quietness, the absence of sound.

sign

silk NOUN a very fine thread used to make a soft, delicate cloth.

silly ADJECTIVE (sillier, silliest) foolish, not sensible.

silver NOUN **1** a precious metal. **2** the colour of this.

since 1 after the time when. *We haven't seen them since they moved.* **2** because. *I must go since it's so late.*

sing VERB (sang, sung) to make music with your voice. *She sings tunefully.*

sink NOUN a basin with taps and a plug-hole, for washing dishes, clothes, etc.

sink VERB (sank, sunk) to go down below a surface. *The boat sank without trace.*

sink

sister

sip VERB (sipping, sipped) to drink by taking only tiny amounts into your mouth at a time.

sister NOUN a girl or woman who has the same parents as you.

sit VERB (sitting, sat) to be in a position where your bottom is on a seat.

sitting-room NOUN room in a home to sit and relax in.

six the number 6.

6
six

sixteen the number 16.

sixty the number 60.

size NOUN **1** how big something is. **2** a particular measurement. *She asked for a dress in size 12.*

skate NOUN **1** a boot or shoe with a blade fitted to the underneath so that you can move on ice. **2** a roller skate.

skate VERB (skating, skated) to move on ice with skates.

skateboard NOUN a board with roller-skate wheels fitted to the underneath.

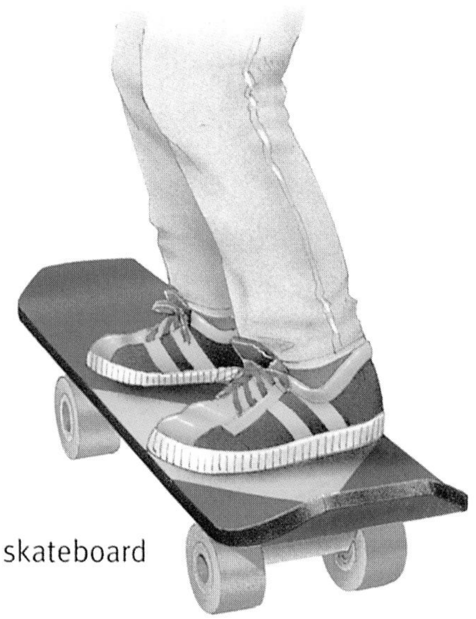
skateboard

skeleton NOUN the framework of bones in your body.

ski VERB to move on snow.

ski

skin NOUN **1** the outer layer of your body. **2** outer covering of a fruit or vegetable.

skip VERB (skipping, skipped) **1** to jump with light, quick steps. **2** to jump over a rope which swings over your head and under your feet.

skirt NOUN a piece of women's clothing that hangs down from the waist.

sky NOUN (PLURAL skies) the space around the earth.

skyscraper NOUN a very tall building in a city.

sledge NOUN a vehicle for moving over snow and ice.

sleep VERB (slept) to rest in bed with your eyes closed and your mind and body in an unconscious state, not to be awake.

sleep

sleet NOUN partly-frozen rain.

sleeve NOUN the part of a garment covering the arm.

slept See **sleep**. *I slept for seven hours last night.*

slice NOUN thin piece of food cut from something larger.

slid See **slide**. *They slid on the ice.*

slide NOUN **1** something with a slippery surface down which you can slide. **2** a picture that can be projected onto a screen. **3** a clip girls wear to keep their hair tidy.

slide VERB (sliding, slid) to move smoothly over a surface.

slip VERB (slipping, slipped) **1** to slide and lose your balance. **2** to make a mistake.

slipper NOUN a light shoe to wear indoors.

slippery ADJECTIVE smooth, wet or greasy and difficult to hold or walk on.

slow ADJECTIVE **1** taking a long time, not fast. **2** behind the right time. *My watch is slow.* **3** not quick to understand.

slug NOUN a creature like a snail, but with no shell.

small ADJECTIVE little, not big.

smash VERB to break into pieces.

smell NOUN the effect of something on your nose.

smell VERB (smelt or smelled) to have a particular smell that you can sense.

smelt or **smelled** *See* **smell**. *I smelt something burning.*

smile VERB (smiling, smiled) to look pleased and happy, often with your mouth turned up at the corners.

smile

smoke NOUN the cloudy gas that is produced when something burns.

smoke VERB (smoking, smoked) to suck tobacco smoke from a cigarette, cigar or pipe into your mouth and let it out again.

smooth ADJECTIVE having an even surface, not rough.

snack NOUN a light meal.

snail NOUN a small creature with a shell on its back.

snake NOUN a long creature with no legs.

sneeze VERB (sneezing, sneezed) to suddenly and noisily let air out of your nose and mouth, as when you have a cold.

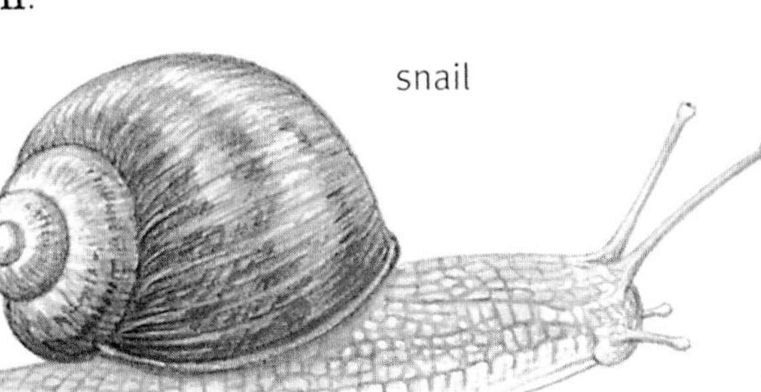

snail

snooker NOUN game in which you use a long stick to hit coloured balls into pockets at the sides of a large table.

snore VERB (snoring, snored) to breathe noisily through your nose and mouth when you are asleep.

snow NOUN flakes of frozen water that fall from the sky in cold weather.

snowflake NOUN one of the soft, white bits of frozen water that fall as snow.

so 1 in the way described. *The house was empty and stayed so for some years.* **2** therefore, in order that. *It was cold, so I lit the fire.*

snake

did you know?

small

Here is a list of adjectives that are used to show how small or big something is. How many of them do you know?

microscopic, miniature, minute, tiny, little, small, big, large, great, colossal, enormous, giant, gigantic, huge, immense, mammoth, massive, vast.

A B C D E F G H I J K L M N O P Q R S T U V W X Y Z

soap NOUN a substance that is used with water for washing.

sock NOUN a piece of clothing that covers your foot and the bottom of your leg and is worn inside shoes.

socket NOUN a hole into which something else fits.

sofa NOUN a comfortable seat for two or more people with a back and arms, a settee.

soft ADJECTIVE **1** not hard. **2** smooth and nice to touch. **3** gentle.

soil NOUN the top layer of the ground in which plants grow.

sofa

sold *See* **sell**. *We sold the car for £500.*

soldier NOUN someone whose job is to fight in an army.

solid ADJECTIVE **1** having a firm shape, not liquid or gas. **2** not hollow inside. **3** of the same material all the way through. *Solid gold.*

some 1 a few, but not all. **2** used when you are not being exact about what you are referring to. *At some point we will have to talk about this.*

did you know?

space

In the 1950s and 1960s Russia and the USA tried to rival each other's achievements in space. They hoped to prove that their nation was the most advanced.

In 1957, Russia took the lead by launching the first satellite and, in 1961, the first manned space flight. But in 1969, the USA won the space race by landing the first man on the moon, Neil Armstrong.

something a thing that is not named, any thing.

sometimes now and then.

son NOUN someone's male child.

song NOUN words sung to music.

soon in a short time.

sore ADJECTIVE painful, aching. *Sore feet.*

sorry ADJECTIVE (sorrier, sorriest) feeling sad, wanting to apologize for something you have said or done. *I'm so sorry.*

sort NOUN a group of things or people of a particular type.

sort VERB to arrange things in order.

sound NOUN anything that you hear.

soup

soup NOUN a liquid food made by boiling meat, vegetables, etc., in water.

sour ADJECTIVE having a sharp taste, not sweet.

south NOUN one of the four points of the compass, the direction that is on your right when you face the rising Sun.

south

space NOUN **1** the universe beyond the Earth's atmosphere. **2** an empty or open area.

spaceship NOUN a vehicle that can travel in space.

spade NOUN a tool for digging with, a kind of shovel.

did you know?

spell

Test your spelling. Which is the correct spelling?

February or Febuary
fourty or forty
friend or freind
library or libary
neice or niece

Look these words up in this dictionary to find the answers!

spaghetti NOUN long strings of pasta.

sparrow NOUN a very common, small brown bird.

speak VERB (spoke, spoken) to talk, to say things.

special ADJECTIVE not ordinary. *She is special.*

speed NOUN how quickly something moves. *Moving at the speed of light.*

spell VERB (spelt or spelled) to put the letters in a word in the right order.

spelt or **spelled** *See* **spell**. *I spelt the words correctly.*

spend VERB (spent) **1** to pay out money. **2** to pass the time. *He liked to spend his time reading.*

spent *See* **spend**. *They spent all the money.*

spice NOUN a powder or seeds of a plant used to flavour food.

spider NOUN a small creature with eight legs that usually spins a web.

spill VERB (spilt or spilled) to pour something out or over something else without meaning to.

spill

spilt or **spilled** *See* **spill**. *Jo spilt the milk.*

spin VERB (spinning, spun) **1** to twist something into a thread. **2** to make something by forming threads. **3** to go round and round very fast.

splash VERB to make a liquid scatter in drops, especially so that it makes someone or something wet.

spoil VERB (spoilt or spoiled) **1** to ruin. **2** to make a child selfish. *You spoil him.*

spider

spoilt or **spoiled** *See* **spoil**. *The bad weather spoilt our holiday.*

spoke, spoken *See* **speak**. *Angela spoke to the man in German.*

spooky ADJECTIVE (spookier, spookiest) something that is strange and frightening. *The old house felt really spooky.*

sponge NOUN **1** something you wash with that soaks up water. **2** a light cake.

spoon NOUN a tool you use to stir, serve and eat food.

sport NOUN games, activities, etc., that you do for pleasure.

spot NOUN **1** a small, round mark, a dot. **2** a pimple. **3** a particular place.

spray VERB to scatter liquid in lots of small drops. *We used the hose to spray water all over the garden.*

splash

spread VERB (spread) **1** to lay something out flat. *We spread the blanket on the ground.* **2** to thinly cover a surface with something. *Spread butter on your toast.* **3** to move out over a wider area. *News of the disaster spread very quickly.*

a b c d e f g h i j k l m n o p q r s t u v w x y z

spring NOUN the season of the year that comes after winter and before summer.

spring

spun *See* **spin**. *The wheels spun fast.*

square NOUN **1** a shape with four equal sides. **2** an open space in a town or city, surrounded by buildings.

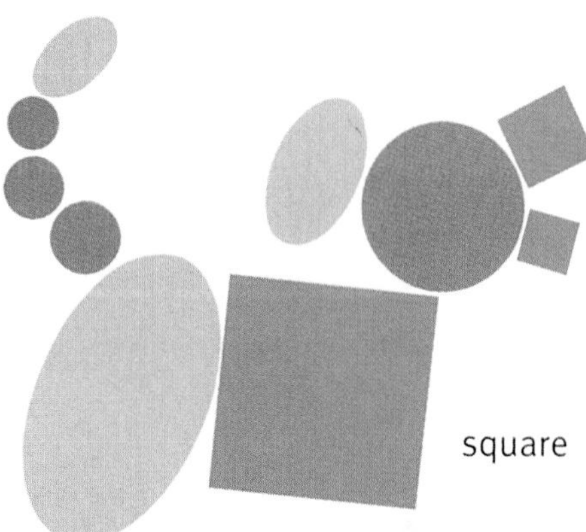

square

squash NOUN **1** lots of people crowded into a small space. **2** a fruit drink. **3** a racket game for two or four players.

squash VERB to crush or squeeze. *Julia squashed the cans for recycling.*

did you know?

star

There are billions of stars scattered through space. Stars look small because they are far away, but most are gigantic glowing balls of gas. They burn from between a few million to tens of billions of years.

squeak VERB to make a short, high-pitched noise.

squeeze VERB (squeezing, squeezed) to press the sides of something together, usually to get liquid out of it or to force it into a smaller space.

squirrel NOUN a small animal that has a bushy tail and which climbs trees.

stable NOUN a building in which horses are kept.

stage NOUN **1** raised platform on which actors perform. **2** a point in the development of someone or something.

stage

stairs PLURAL NOUN a series of steps in a building that lead from one floor to the next.

stamp

stamp NOUN **1** a small piece of paper that you must stick onto a letter before you post it. **2** a small device that prints words or signs on paper.

stamp VERB **1** to hit the ground with your foot. **2** to print a mark with a stamp. **3** to put a postage stamp on an envelope.

stand VERB (stood) to be upright on your feet.

star NOUN **1** one of the small, bright points of light you can see in the sky at night. **2** a shape with five or six points. **3** a famous entertainer.

stare VERB (staring, stared) to look at someone or something for a long time without blinking. *I stared at the picture on the wall.*

start VERB to begin. *I always start my exercise class with some stretches.*

did you know?

stamp

The first postage stamp was the Penny Black, which appeared in Britain for the first time in 1840. It showed a portrait of Queen Victoria on a black background, and cost one penny.

station NOUN **1** a building on a railway or bus route where you begin or end a journey. **2** a building that is a centre for a particular service. *A fire station.*

stay VERB **1** to stop and remain. **2** to be a guest. *We stayed in a hotel for the weekend.*

steal VERB (stole,'stolen) to take something that belongs to someone else without their permission.

steam NOUN the gas produced when water boils.

steep ADJECTIVE rising or falling sharply.

steep

stem NOUN the part of a plant above the ground on which the leaves and flowers grow.

stem

step NOUN **1** the act of putting one foot in front of the other when you are walking. **2** a flat surface that you put your foot on to go up or down to a different level. **3** one of a series of actions you take when making or doing something. **4** (steps) a stepladder, one that is hinged so that it stands up by itself.

step-mother/father NOUN the person who your father/ mother has remarried.

stick NOUN **1** a long, thin piece of wood. **2** a thin piece of anything. *A stick of rock.*

stick VERB (stuck) to fix together with glue.

still ADJECTIVE not moving.

sting NOUN **1** the part of an insect's body that it uses as a weapon. **2** the painful wound caused by the poison from an insect's sting.

sting VERB (stung) to cause a painful wound and swelling in a part of your body.

stir VERB (stirring, stirred) to mix something by moving it round with something such as a spoon.

stocking NOUN a piece of women's clothing that fits over the foot and leg.

stole, stolen *See* **steal**. *The thief stole the jewels.*

stomach NOUN the part inside your body where your food is digested.

stone NOUN **1** a piece of rock. **2** the hard seed inside some fruits such as cherries or peaches. **3** a measurement of weight equal to 14 pounds or 6.35 kilograms.

stood *See* **stand**. *The children stood up.*

stool NOUN seat with three or four legs but no back or arms.

stool

stop VERB (stopping, stopped) **1** to come to a standstill. **2** to prevent.

store NOUN **1** a collection of things for future use. **2** a place to keep things. **3** a large shop.

store VERB (storing, stored) to put something away for future use.

storm NOUN bad weather, usually with thunder, lightning and heavy rain.

storm

story NOUN (PLURAL stories) an account of something real or imaginary.

straight 1 in a straight line. **2** directly. *Go straight there.*

straight ADJECTIVE not bent. *Straight hair.*

strange ADJECTIVE unusual, odd. *A strange taste.*

straw NOUN **1** the dried stems of plants like wheat that are used for animal bedding, or for making mats and baskets. **2** a thin tube that you suck a drink through.

strawberry NOUN (PLURAL strawberries) a soft, juicy, red fruit.

stream NOUN a small, narrow river. *There are tadpoles in the stream.*

street NOUN road in a town or village with houses along it. *High Street.*

strength NOUN power, energy. *Superhuman strength.*

stretch VERB **1** to make something bigger by pulling it. **2** to reach out. **3** to hold your arms and legs out straight and tighten your muscles.

strict ADJECTIVE severe in matters of discipline and rules of behaviour.

string NOUN **1** strong thread used for tying things. **2** one of the wires or threads stretched over a musical instrument, tennis racket, etc.

strip NOUN a long, narrow piece of land, cloth, etc.

stripe NOUN one band of colour in between others.

strong ADJECTIVE powerful, not easy to break.

stuck *See* **stick**. *The pieces of the aircraft kit were stuck together.*

study VERB (studying, studied) to spend your time learning about a subject.

stung *See* **sting**. *I was stung by a wasp.*

submarine NOUN a type of ship that can travel underwater.

subtract VERB to take away a number or amount from a larger number or amount.

subway NOUN a path for you to walk on that goes underneath a busy road.

string

such 1 so much. *We're such good friends.* **2** like. *People such as you and me.*

suck VERB **1** to draw in liquid or air. **2** to eat something by melting it in your mouth as you move it round with your tongue. *Suck an ice lolly.*

suddenly happening very quickly and unexpectedly.

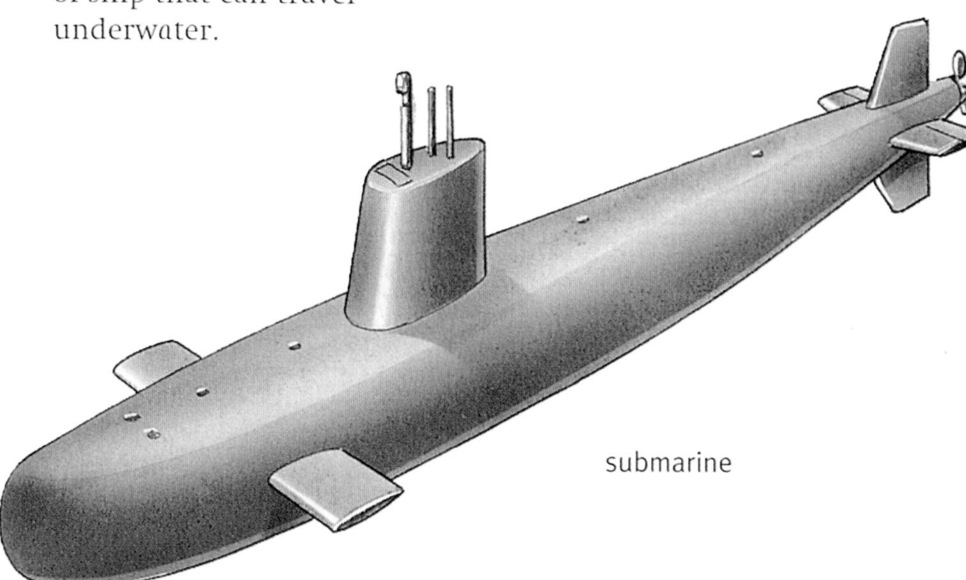

submarine

sugar NOUN a sweetener for food and drinks.

sugar cane

suit NOUN a set of matching clothes. *Trouser suit.*

suitcase NOUN a case for carrying your belongings in when you are travelling.

sum NOUN an exercise in simple arithmetic.

summer NOUN the season of the year that comes after spring and before autumn.

summer

sun NOUN the bright star that gives heat and light during the day. *The earth goes round the Sun and that gives us heat and light.*

Sunday NOUN the day of the week before Monday.

did you know?

suffix

- A *suffix* is a group of letters that you add to the end of a word to make a new word.

  For example *-ly* is added to many adjectives to make adverbs, for example: *soft – softly*.

  Other examples:

  -ful, meaning 'full of': *joy – joyful*;
  -ness, to make a noun: *kind – kindness*.
- See also ***prefix***.

sunflower NOUN a plant that can grow to be very tall. It has a very large flower with yellow petals.

sung *See* **sing**. *The songs were sung well by the children.*

sunk *See* **sink**. *The 'Titanic' was sunk by an iceberg.*

sunny ADJECTIVE (sunnier, sunniest) brightly lit by the sun. *It was a sunny day.*

sunrise NOUN the rising of the sun at the beginning of the day, dawn.

sunset NOUN the going down of the Sun at the end of the day.

supermarket NOUN a large, self-service shop which sells lots of different foods and other goods.

supper NOUN the last meal of the day.

sure ADJECTIVE without doubt, certain.

surface NOUN the outside or top of something.

surgery NOUN (PLURAL surgeries) the place where doctors or dentists see their patients.

did you know?

sun

The Sun is a middle-aged star. It is thought that it was formed five billion years ago. It is the centre of our solar system and is said to weigh just under 2,000 trillion, trillion tons!

sunrise

surprise NOUN an unexpected event. *Surprise party.*

swallow NOUN an insect-eating bird with a forked tail. *Swallows on the telegraph wires.*

swallow VERB to make food pass from your mouth down your throat.

swam *See* **swim**. *I swam three lengths.*

swamp NOUN waterlogged land, a bog or marsh.

swamp VERB to overwhelm, flood. *The radio station was swamped with complaints.*

swan NOUN a large, usually white bird with a long neck that lives on rivers and lakes.

swap NOUN something given in exchange for something else. *This stamp is a swap.*

swap VERB (swapping, swapped) to exchange one thing for another. *He swapped his football for a cricket bat.*

swat VERB (swatting, swatted) to hit with a sharp blow. *He swatted the fly with a newspaper, but missed.*

sway VERB **1** to lean in one direction and then another. *He swayed from side to side.* **2** to be uncertain.

sweater NOUN a woollen garment for the top part of your body, a pullover.

sweep VERB (swept) to brush clean. *Dan swept the leaves from the path.*

sweet ADJECTIVE **1** sugary to the taste. *The tea tasted sweet.* **2** kind and pleasant. *She is very sweet.*

swallow

swan

sweet NOUN a small, sweet, sugary item to eat, such as a toffee, chocolate or mint.

sweet pea NOUN a climbing plant which often has sweet-smelling flowers.

sweep

swell VERB (swells, swelled, swollen) to grow larger, to expand. *He swelled with pride.*

swell NOUN **1** the process of swelling. **2** the rise and fall of the sea's surface.

did you know?

swans

There are seven different species of swans. Four of these species live in the northern hemisphere and have white feathers over their entire bodies. The other three species are found in the southern hemisphere and have some black feathers.

Swans are among the heaviest birds able to fly. But they need a long, clear stretch of water to take off.

swelling NOUN a part of the body that has swollen. *There was a swelling on his neck.*

swept *See* **sweep**. *I swept the floor.*

swim VERB (swimming, swam, swum) to travel through water by moving your arms and legs. *I go swimming every Monday evening.*

swim

swimming costume NOUN a tight-fitting garment that women and girls wear when they go swimming.

swimming pool NOUN a pool made for people to swim in.

did you know?

syllable

- A *syllable* is a part of a word which contains a single vowel sound and is said as a unit.
- The vowel sound may be spelt with more than one letter.
- A syllable may contain one or more consonant sounds.
- The words in the following examples are divided into syllables:

  book, head, quick-ly, car-di-gan, in-for-ma-tion.

swimming trunks NOUN the shorts that men and boys wear when they swim.

swing NOUN a seat hanging from ropes or chains that you can sit on and swing.

swing VERB (swung) to repeatedly move backwards and forwards or from side to side from a fixed point.

switch NOUN a control for turning electricity on and off.

swivel (swivels, swivelling, swivelled) VERB to turn round. *I swivelled in amazement.*

swoop VERB to come down with a rush. *The eagle swooped on its prey.*

sword NOUN weapon with a handle and long, sharp blade.

swordfish NOUN a large seafish with a long upper jaw that looks like a sword.

swum *See* **swim**. *Three people have swum the Channel.*

swung *See* **swing**. *The soldiers swung their arms as they marched.*

did you know?

synonym

- A *synonym* is a word that has a very similar meaning to another word.
- For example, *weak – feeble; little – small; strong – powerful.*
- See also ***antonym***.

syringe NOUN instrument for injecting liquids into the body.

syringe VERB to clean with a syringe. *I had my ears syringed.*

sword

syrup NOUN a thick sweet liquid. *Golden syrup.*

syrupy ADJECTIVE very sweet, like syrup.

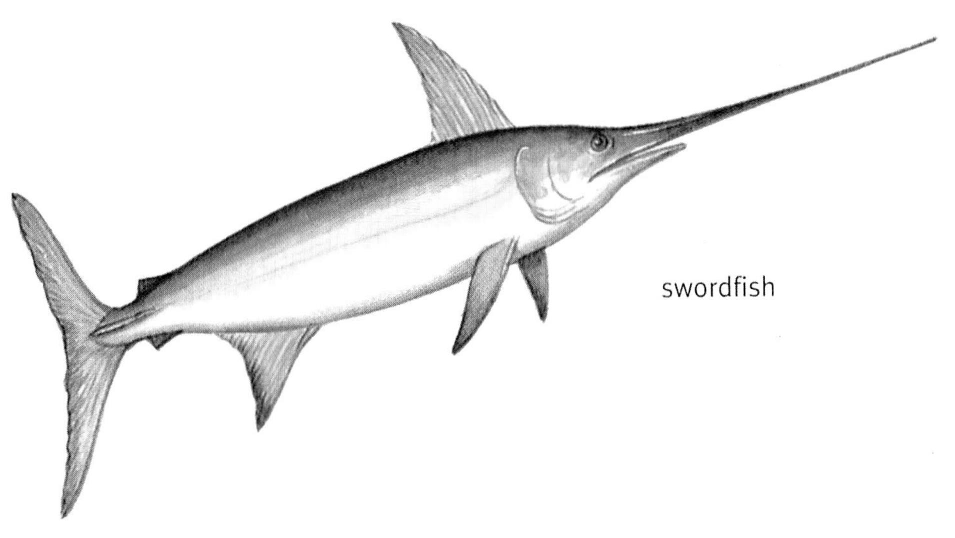

swordfish

Tt

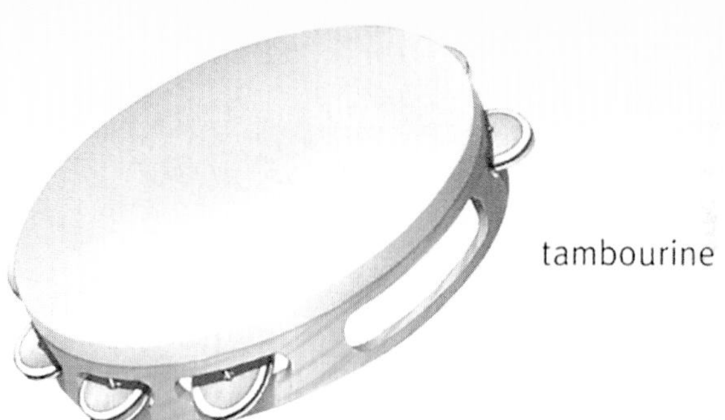

tambourine

table NOUN **1** a piece of furniture with legs that support a flat top. **2** a set of figures arranged in order. *Times tables.*

table tennis NOUN an indoor game in which two or four players hit a light ball backwards and forwards across a low net on a table, ping pong.

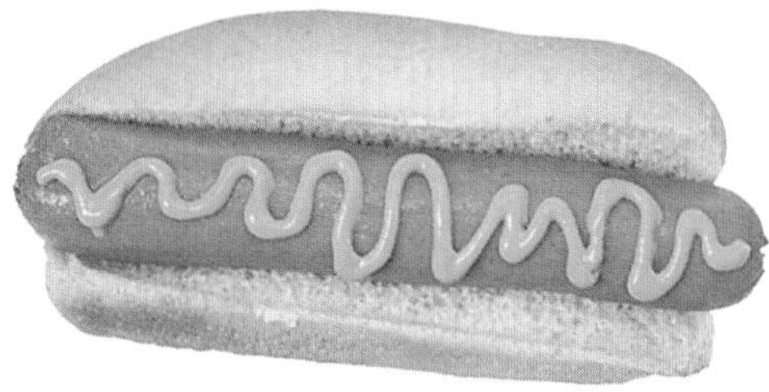

take-away

tablet NOUN a small piece of solid medicine, a pill.

tadpole NOUN the young of a frog or toad.

tail NOUN the part at the back of an animal, bird or fish.

take VERB (taking, took, taken) **1** to get hold of something. *Take my hand.* **2** to carry or remove. *Let me take your coat.* **3** to have or use. *Do you take sugar in your tea?* **4** to travel in a vehicle. *Take a taxi.* **5** to need. *How long will it take to do your homework?* **6** to steal. *Someone has taken my money.*

take-away NOUN food bought to eat at home.

taken See **take**. *Who has taken my bag?*

tale NOUN a story.

talk VERB to speak, to have a conversation.

tall ADJECTIVE **1** higher than average. *A tall glass.* **2** having a particular height. *The tree was 20 metres tall.*

tambourine NOUN a small drum with metal discs round the edge.

tame ADJECTIVE not fierce or wild.

tank NOUN **1** a large metal container for holding liquids or gas. **2** an armoured vehicle.

tap NOUN a device that you turn to control the flow of liquid, gas, etc., from a pipe or container.

tape NOUN **1** a narrow strip of ribbon, paper, etc. **2** a strip of plastic covered with a magnetic material and used to record sound, pictures, computer data, etc.

tape VERB (taping, taped) to record sound, pictures, computer data, etc., on magnetic tape.

tart NOUN pastry case with a sweet or savoury filling.

taste VERB (tasting, tasted) to use your tongue to feel the flavour of something.

tasty ADJECTIVE having a pleasant taste.

taught See **teach**. *Mr Peacock taught our class last year.*

taxi NOUN a car with a driver who you pay to take you somewhere. *Call a taxi.*

taxi

tea NOUN **1** a hot drink. *Make a cup of tea.* **2** a meal that you eat in the afternoon or early evening.

teabag NOUN a small bag filled with tea leaves that you pour boiling water on to make a drink of tea.

teach VERB (taught) to train someone in the knowledge of a subject or skill, to give lessons. *I teach Sophie how to play tennis.*

teacher NOUN a person whose job is to teach. *My maths teacher gave me good marks.*

team NOUN a group of people who play on the same side in a game or who work on something together. *The netball team.*

teapot

teapot NOUN a container with a lid, handle and spout, that you use for making and pouring tea.

tear (said like **beer**) NOUN a drop of salty water that comes from your eyes when you cry. *Helena burst into tears.*

tear (said like **bare**) VERB (tore, torn) to pull to pieces. *Tear the paper into strips.*

tease VERB (teasing, teased) to make fun of someone.

teaspoon NOUN a small spoon that you use to stir tea or coffee.

teeth *See* **tooth**.

telephone NOUN the electrical system or the piece of equipment that you use to dial a number and talk to someone in another place.

telescope NOUN instrument that helps you to see objects that are far away more clearly.

television NOUN **1** the sending of sound and pictures over radio waves. **2** the piece of electrical equipment that receives these.

tell VERB (told) **1** to make something known by speaking about it, to pass on information. **2** to decide or find out.

tear

temperature NOUN how hot or cold something is.

ten the number 10.

10

ten

tennis NOUN a game for two or four people in which a ball is hit with rackets over a net on a court.

tent NOUN a movable shelter for camping out in, made of canvas or nylon stretched over a framework of poles and fixed down with ropes.

term NOUN **1** one of the periods of time that the school year is divided into. **2** a condition of an agreement.

terrible ADJECTIVE very bad or frightening. *Rachel had a terrible experience.*

test NOUN a set of questions to measure your knowledge, an examination. *My sister is taking her driving test.*

than used when you compare two things or people. *I like this dress better than that one.*

thank VERB to tell someone that you are grateful for something they have done, said, or given to you. *I thanked my parents for the presents. My sister always thanks the vet for his help.*

that 1 used in joining a sentence. **2** who or which. *The house that Jack built.* **3** (PLURAL those) the one there, the one described. *That dog bit me.* **4** to such an amount. *His jokes weren't that funny.*

the 1 used to refer to that particular thing or person. *The queen.* **2** used to refer to the only people or things of that type. *The media. The poor.*

theatre NOUN **1** a building with a stage where plays, etc., are performed. **2** a room in a hospital where operations are carried out.

their belonging to them.

theirs that or those belonging to them.

them *See* **they**. *I like them.*

themselves *See* **they**. *They helped themselves to sweets.*

theme park NOUN an amusement park where the rides and activities are based round a single theme.

did you know?

theatre

Theatres first appeared in ancient Greece. They were in the open air, built on hillsides so the audience could see the players. In Britain, the first theatres were on the backs of the carts that the actors travelled in!

More recently, theatres have been built with proper walls and roofs. They can be very grand and richly-furnished.

then 1 at that time. *There were no motorways then.* **2** next, afterwards. *We had dinner and then went for a drink.* **3** if that is the case. *If you know the answer, then put your hand up.*

there 1 in or at that place. *We're nearly there.* **2** used at the beginning of a sentence with a verb like 'be'. *There is no hope.*

there's = there is, there has. *There's been an accident.*

thermometer NOUN an instrument for measuring temperature.

thermometer

Thermos NOUN (trademark) a container to keep drinks hot.

these *See* **this**. *These books.*

they (them, themselves) **1** the ones described. **2** used instead of 'he' or 'she'. *If anyone phones, tell them to call back later.*

they'd = they had, they would. *They'd forgotten her birthday present.*

they'll = they will. *They'll be here soon.*

they're = they are. *They're back!*

they've = they have. *They've gone.*

thick ADJECTIVE **1** not thin. **2** measuring a particular amount. *The castle walls were a metre thick.* **3** not watery. *Thick gravy.* **4** difficult to see through. *Thick fog.*

thief NOUN (PLURAL thieves) someone who steals.

thieves *See* **thief**.

thin ADJECTIVE (thinner, thinnest) **1** narrow, not thick. **2** not fat. *A thin girl.* **3** watery. *Thin soup.*

think VERB (thought) to use your mind, to have an idea or opinion.

third ADJECTIVE the one after the second, 3rd.

thirsty ADJECTIVE (thirstier, thirstiest) wanting or needing a drink.

thirteen the number 13. *Unlucky thirteen.*

thirty the number 30.

this (PLURAL these) the one here. *This is a good book.*

thorn NOUN sharp prickle growing on a plant like a rose. *Gareth pricked his finger on a thorn.*

thorn

those *See* **that**. *Those animals.*

thought NOUN an idea or opinion

thought *See* **think**. *I thought about our holiday last year.*

thousand NOUN the number 1,000.

thread NOUN **1** a long, thin piece of cotton or nylon used with a needle when sewing. **2** a long, thin length of any other material. **3** a raised line that winds round the outside of a screw.

three the number **3**.

threw *See* **throw**. *Jack threw the ball.*

throat NOUN **1** the part of your body at the front of your neck. **2** the tube in your neck that takes air to your lungs and food to your stomach.

through 1 from one end or side to the other. *We drove through the village.* **2** from beginning to end. *All through the winter.* **3** by means of. *We got in through the window.* **4** because of. *I dropped the jug through carelessness.*

throw VERB (threw, thrown) to send something through the air by a movement of your arm.

thrown *See* **throw**. *How far have you thrown the ball?*

thumb NOUN the short, thick finger on the side of your hand.

thunder NOUN the loud noise that follows lightning.

Thursday NOUN the day of the week after Wednesday and before Friday.

ticket NOUN a piece of paper or card to show that you have paid to go on or into something.

ticket

tickle VERB (tickling, tickled) to touch someone lightly to make them laugh.

tide NOUN the regular rising and falling of the sea.

tie NOUN **1** a piece of clothing worn under the collar of a shirt and knotted at the front. **2** an equal score in a game or competition.

tie VERB (tying, tied) **1** to fasten or knot with string, rope, etc. **2** to finish a game or competition with equal points.

tiger

tiger NOUN a large animal of the cat family that is yellow-brown with black stripes.

tight ADJECTIVE **1** fastened very firmly. **2** fitting very close to the body, not loose. *My trousers feel very tight, I don't think that they fit me anymore.*

tights PLURAL NOUN a close-fitting garment that covers all the lower half of the body.

till until. *I can play till tea.*

till NOUN a machine that has a drawer for money and adds up the prices in a shop.

time NOUN **1** the passing of hours, days, weeks, years, etc. **2** a particular moment in the day. *Teatime.* **3** a period or occasion. *We had a good time.* **4** the speed and beat of a piece of music. *She can dance in time to the music.*

tin NOUN **1** a soft metal. **2** a metal box or container.

tiny ADJECTIVE (tinier, tiniest) very small.

tip NOUN **1** the end of something. **2** a small amount of money that you give to someone who does you a service. **3** a helpful piece of advice. **4** a place where rubbish is dumped.

tip VERB (tipping, tipped) **1** to put something onto one edge so that it overturns. **2** to give someone a tip.

tiptoe VERB to move on your toes, especially when you are trying not to make a noise.

tired ADJECTIVE feeling that you need to rest or sleep.

tissue NOUN a paper handkerchief.

to 1 in the direction of, towards. *A train to Manchester.* **2** as far as. *We came to the end of the road.* **3** against. *Back to back.* **4** compared with. *I prefer drawing to painting.*

toad NOUN animal like a frog.

toast NOUN bread browned in a toaster or under a grill.

toaster NOUN a machine that heats bread so that it goes crisp and brown.

toboggan NOUN a light sledge.

today this present day.

toboggan

tiptoe

toddler NOUN a child who has just learnt to walk.

toe NOUN one of the five parts of your body at the end of your foot.

toffee NOUN a hard, sticky sweet.

together 1 joined into one piece, group, etc. **2** all at the same time.

toilet NOUN a lavatory.

told *See* **tell**. *The teacher told us a story.*

tomato NOUN (PLURAL tomatoes) a round, juicy, red fruit eaten raw or cooked.

tomorrow the day after today. *I am going to my best friend's birthday party tomorrow.*

tongue NOUN the part in your mouth with which you taste things.

too 1 also, as well. *I went on holiday to France and my parents came too.* **2** more than you need or want. *The food looked so delicious that we all ate far too much at Christmas.*

took *See* **take**. *Jo took Sam's favourite book.*

tool NOUN an instrument that you use to do a job.

tooth NOUN (PLURAL teeth) **1** one of a row of white, bony parts in your mouth that you use to bite your food. **2** one of a row of pointed bits on things such as a comb, zip, saw, etc.

toothbrush NOUN a small brush for cleaning your teeth.

tomato

top NOUN **1** the highest point or position. **2**. The highest part of something. **3** a spinning toy. **4** a piece of clothing that you wear on the upper part of your body.

torch NOUN battery-operated light that you carry in your hand.

tore, torn *See* **tear**. *Someone has torn my coat.*

tortoise NOUN a slow-moving animal with a hard shell covering its body.

total NOUN the complete amount when everything is added up together.

touch VERB **1** to feel with your hands. **2** to be against something. **3** to be moved in your feelings.

towel NOUN a piece of paper or cloth used for drying things.

tower NOUN a tall building or a tall part of a building.

town NOUN a place with a large number of houses, shops, etc.

toy NOUN something that a child plays with.

toy

track NOUN **1** a rough path. **2** the mark left by tyres, footprints, etc. **3** a railway line. **4** a single piece of music on a tape or disc.

tractor NOUN a vehicle used on farms.

tortoise

traffic NOUN the moving vehicles on roads, motorways, etc.

train NOUN a line of railway carriages pulled by an engine.

trainers PLURAL NOUN sports shoes.

trampoline

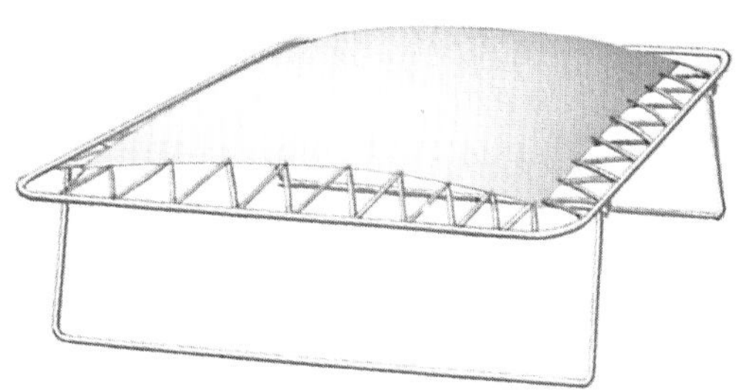

trampoline NOUN a large piece of canvas held by springs in a frame for jumping on.

travel VERB (travelling, travelled) to go from one place to another, to go on a journey.

tray NOUN a flat board with raised edges that you can carry things on.

tread VERB (trod, trodden) to put your foot on the ground, as when you walk.

treasure NOUN a store of valuable and precious things.

tree NOUN a tall plant with a trunk and branches.

triangle NOUN **1** a shape with three sides. **2** a musical instrument in this shape.

trick NOUN **1** something done to deceive you. **2** a clever action done to amuse you.

trick VERB to make someone believe something that is not true.

tricycle NOUN a vehicle with three wheels, especially a child's toy.

trip VERB (tripping, tripped) to stumble and lose your balance.

trod, trodden *See* **tread**. *He trod on the beetle.*

trousers PLURAL NOUN a piece of clothing that fastens at the waist and covers each leg separately.

truck NOUN a lorry or heavy goods vehicle.

true ADJECTIVE correct, real, not false.

trumpet NOUN a musical instrument that you blow into.

did you know?

tree

How many of these different trees do you know? Ash, beech, birch, cedar, chestnut, cypress, Dutch elm, elm, fig, fir, hawthorn, horse chestnut, larch, laurel, lime, maple, monkey puzzle, oak, palm, pine, plane, poplar, rowan, silver birch, sycamore, weeping willow, yew.

trunk NOUN **1** the main stem of a tree. **2** the main part of your body. **3** the long nose of an elephant. **4** a large box to put your things in when you are travelling.

trust VERB to believe in and depend on the goodness of someone.

truth NOUN whatever is true.

try VERB (trying, tried) **1** to make an effort to do something. **2** to test something out. **3** to examine someone in a court of law.

trunk

tube NOUN **1** a round, hollow length of metal, plastic, rubber, etc. **2** a small, soft container that holds things like toothpaste, cream or paint.

Tuesday NOUN the day of the week after Monday and before Wednesday.

tulip NOUN a spring flower that grows from a bulb.

tumble VERB (tumbling, tumbled) to take a sudden fall.

tumble dryer NOUN a machine to dry wet clothes.

tuna NOUN a large fish used as food.

tunnel NOUN a long passage under the ground or under water.

tunnel

turkey NOUN a large bird kept on farms for its meat.

turn VERB **1** to move round, like a wheel. **2** to change direction. *Turn to face the front of the class.* **3** to become. *To turn blue with cold.* **4** to use a control to do something. *Turn the television off.*

turquoise NOUN a bluish-green colour.

twelve the number 12.

tulip

twenty the number 20.

twig NOUN a thin stem on a branch.

twin NOUN **1** either of two children born to the same mother at the same time. **2** one of two things exactly the same. *Twin beds.*

twist VERB **1** to wind threads together. **2** to turn and pull a part of your body so that it hurts. *Twist your ankle.* **3** to curve. *The road twisted and turned down the mountain.*

two the number 2.

typewriter

typewriter NOUN a machine with a keyboard for printing letters onto paper.

tyre NOUN a rubber tube filled with air that fits round the outside of a wheel.

did you know?

too

Which of the spellings of the words to, too, and two are correct?

I want *to/too/two* go now.

You can come *to/too/two*.

I have *to/too/two* hands.

Uu

umbrella

ugly ADJECTIVE (uglier, ugliest) not attractive to look at.

umbrella NOUN a piece of nylon stretched over a folding frame that keeps the rain off you when you put it up.

uncle NOUN **1** the brother of your mother or father. **2** the husband of your aunt.

under 1 below, lower than. *Under the bed.* **2** less than. *Reductions for children under 16.* **3** in the process of. *New ideas under discussion.* **4** subject to, obeying. *Under starter's orders.*

underground ADJECTIVE below the ground. Rabbits live underground in burrows.

underground NOUN an underground railway. *The London Underground.*

underneath under something else. *I looked underneath the bed for my slippers.*

did you know?

umbrella

From its origin, the word umbrella means 'little shade' or 'little shadow'. This was because it was originally used as a sunshade to give protection from the heat of the sun, rather than to give protection from the rain.

understand VERB (understood) to know what someone is saying or what they mean.

understood *See* **understand**. *I understood what I had to do.*

underwear NOUN clothes that you wear next to your skin, but underneath other clothes.

undress VERB to take your clothes off.

unhappy

unhappy ADJECTIVE (unhappier, unhappiest) sad.

uniform NOUN the special clothing worn by a particular group of people, such as police officers, nurses or schoolchildren.

universe NOUN all of space and everything that exists.

untidy ADJECTIVE (untidier, untidiest) not neat and tidy.

unusual ADJECTIVE strange, not normal or usual.

up 1 to an upright position. *Stand up.* **2** to a higher place. *Climb up the ladder.* **3** at an end. *Your time is up.* **4** along. *Up the road.*

upon on.

upset VERB (upsetting, upset) **1** to tip over, to spill. **2** to make someone unhappy.

upside-down 1 in a position where the top is at the bottom and the bottom is at the top. **2** in an untidy mess.

us *See* **we**. *Come and visit us.*

use VERB (using, used) **1** to do something with a thing. *I shall use the saw to cut wood.* **2** to have done something often in the past. *We used to sit over there.*

upside-down

Vv

vacuum cleaner NOUN a machine that sucks up dust and dirt from carpets.

valley NOUN a lower area of land between mountains or hills, especially with a river running through it.

valley

valuable ADJECTIVE worth a lot of money.

van NOUN a vehicle for carrying goods.

vase NOUN a container to put flowers in or use as an ornament.

vegetable NOUN a plant used for food.

Velcro NOUN (trademark) a fastening for clothes, shoes, etc., in which two nylon strips stick together when you press them against each another.

violin

very especially, most.

vest NOUN a piece of underwear worn on the upper part of your body, usually for extra warmth.

vet NOUN an animal doctor.

vicar NOUN a priest in the Anglican church.

video NOUN **1** a film or other recording that you watch by playing it through your television set. **2** a machine for recording television programmes and playing videos.

video VERB to make a video recording of something.

video camera NOUN a camera that records film onto video tape.

video game NOUN an electronic game played on a computer.

view NOUN **1** something that you see, a scene. *A view of the sea.* **2** an opinion or attitude.

village NOUN a small group of houses and other buildings, but not as big as a town.

vinegar NOUN a sour liquid used to flavour food, especially chips.

violent ADJECTIVE behaving in a way that causes great harm.

violet NOUN **1** a bluish-purple colour. **2** a small purple or white spring flower.

violin NOUN a musical instrument with four strings that is played with a bow.

visit VERB to go to see a person or place and stay there for a time.

visitor NOUN someone who visits a person or place.

voice NOUN the sound that you make when you speak or sing.

volcano NOUN (PLURAL volcanoes) a mountain that sprays out lava and steam through an opening at the top or in the sides.

vote VERB (voting, voted) to choose what you prefer by putting a mark on a piece of paper, raising your hand, etc.

did you know?

verb

- A *verb* is a 'doing' word. It tells us what is happening or being. Examples of verbs are: *go, play, think*.

vowel

- A *vowel* is a sound made by the letters *a, e, i, o* or *u* or by a combination of these letters.

Ww

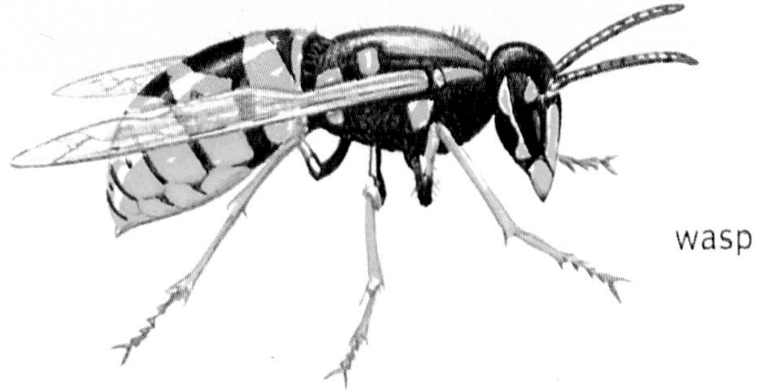
wasp

wagon NOUN *a* truck for heavy loads that is pulled by horses, railway engines, etc.

wait VERB to stay in a place until an expected event happens.

wake VERB (waking, woke or waked, woken or waked) to make or become conscious again after being asleep.

walk VERB to move by putting one foot in front of the other.

wall NOUN **1** a barrier of brick or stone. **2** the side of a room or building.

wallet NOUN a small, flat case for keeping paper money in.

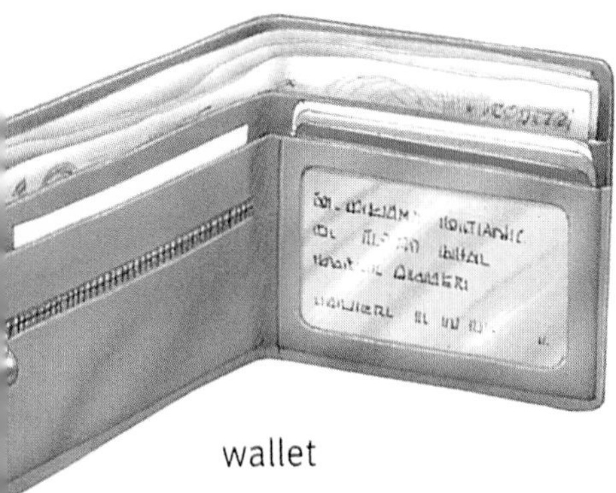
wallet

wand NOUN a thin rod, especially one that you do magic tricks with.

want VERB to need or wish for something. *I want a bicycle for my birthday.*

war NOUN a period of fighting between countries or peoples.

ward NOUN a room in a hospital which has beds for patients.

wardrobe NOUN a cupboard for hanging your clothes in.

warm ADJECTIVE **1** quite hot. *A warm day.* **2** able to keep in the heat. *A warm coat.*

warn VERB to tell someone in advance about a possible danger, result, etc.

was *See* **be**. *The party was good.*

wasn't = was not. *I wasn't sure.*

wash VERB to clean with water.

washing machine NOUN a machine for washing clothes.

wasp NOUN a stinging insect like a bee.

waste NOUN things that are used, damaged, etc., rubbish.

waste VERB (wasting, wasted) to use too much of something when it is not needed. *To waste time.*

watch NOUN a small clock to wear on your wrist.

watch VERB **1** to look at carefully. **2** to take care of.

water NOUN the clear liquid found in rivers and seas that is needed for people and animals to live.

waterfall NOUN a flow of water where a river falls straight over the edge of a cliff or a big rock.

wave NOUN **1** a ridge on the surface of the sea caused by the tide or by the wind. **2** a movement of your hand. **3** the way in which some forms of energy move.

wave VERB (waving, waved) to move your hand to greet someone or to attract their attention.

way NOUN **1** a road, path, lane, etc. *The Fosse Way.* **2** the right direction to follow. *The way out.* **3** how something is done. *The way to make tea.*

we (us, ourselves) the people speaking.

we'd = we had, we would. *We'd better go.*

waterfall

A B C D E F G H I J K L M N O P Q R S T U V W X Y Z

we'll = we will. *We'll come again.*

we're = we are. *We're very happy.*

we've = we have. *We've had a nice time.*

weak ADJECTIVE not strong.

wear VERB (wore, worn) **1** to dress in something. **2** to damage something because it is always being used. *Wear a hole in the carpet.* **3** to last. *These shoes have worn well.*

weather NOUN the conditions of sun, rain, temperature, etc., at a particular time.

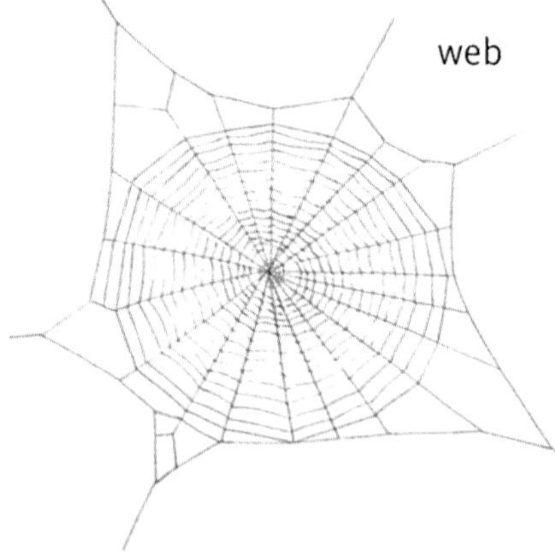

web

web NOUN **1** the network of threads that spiders spin. **2** the piece of skin between the toes of water birds, like ducks. **3** a computer information system on the Internet. *The World Wide Web.*

wedding NOUN a marriage service and the celebrations that follow it.

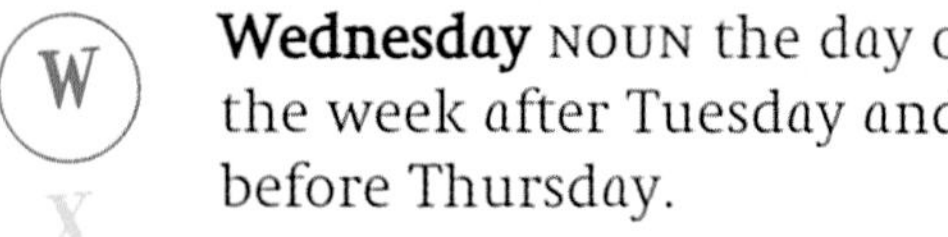

Wednesday NOUN the day of the week after Tuesday and before Thursday.

weed NOUN a wild plant growing where it is not wanted.

week NOUN a period of time equal to seven days and nights.

weep VERB (wept) to cry.

weigh VERB **1** to measure how heavy something or someone is. **2** to have a particular weight.

weight NOUN a measure of how heavy something or someone is.

well 1 in good health. **2** in a good or right way. *He did his job well.*

well NOUN a deep hole dug in the ground to reach water or oil.

went *See* **go**. *Chris went home.*

wept *See* **weep**. *They wept at the sad news.*

were *See* **be**. *They were happy.*

weren't = were not. *You weren't here.*

west NOUN one of the four points of the compass, the direction of the setting Sun.

west

wet ADJECTIVE (wetter, wettest) not dry. *I always get wet when it rains.*

whale NOUN the largest animal that lives in the sea.

did you know?

Wednesday

The name of the day *Wednesday* is in honour of the god *Woden*, the god of wisdom, culture and war. He was the same as the Scandinavian god Odin and the Roman god Mercury.

what 1 which thing or person? **2** to what extent? **3** that which. *I did exactly what he said.*

wheat NOUN a plant producing grains that are made into flour.

wheel NOUN **1** a round object that turns on an axle to move a vehicle, work a machine, etc. **2** a steering wheel.

wheelbarrow NOUN a small cart that has one wheel at the front and two legs and handles at the back which is used for carrying things.

wheelchair NOUN a chair on wheels so that people who cannot walk are able to move.

whale

when 1 at what time? *When are you going shopping?* **2** at the time at which. *It was late when we went to bed.*

where 1 at or in what place? *Where are my gloves?* **2** at, in or to which. *I'm going where the Sun is shining.*

which 1 what person or thing? *Which boy do you mean?* **2** the one or ones that. *The game which we are playing.*

while during the time that. *I went to work while you were still asleep.*

whisker NOUN one of the hairs growing on both sides of a cat's mouth.

whisper VERB to speak to someone so quietly that other people cannot hear.

whisper

whistle NOUN **1** a small, metal tube that gives a loud, shrill sound when you blow into it. **2** a sound that you make when you force your breath out from between your lips.

white

white ADJECTIVE having the colour of snow.

who (whom, whose) **1** which person? **2** the person that. *The boy who shouts the loudest.*

whole ADJECTIVE **1** the complete thing or amount. **2** in one piece.

whom, whose *See* **who**. *Whose shoe is this?*

why for what reason? *Why are you late?*

wide ADJECTIVE **1** large from side to side, not narrow. **2** completely. *She left the window wide open.*

width NOUN the measurement of something from side to side.

wife NOUN (PLURAL wives) the woman a man is married to.

wild ADJECTIVE living in a free and natural way, not tame.

will NOUN **1** the power that you have in your mind to decide what you do. **2** a desire. *The will to win.* **3** a piece of paper that says what you want to do with your possessions when you die.

will used when referring to the future. *I hope you will come to my party.*

win VERB (winning, won) to be the first or best in a competition, game, etc.

wind NOUN a current of air blowing across the surface of the earth.

wind

windmill NOUN **1** a tall building with sails on the outside that turn in the wind to work the machines inside so that grain is crushed into flour. **2** a toy on a stick that blows round in the wind.

window NOUN an opening in a building with glass over it that lets in light and air.

wine NOUN an alcoholic drink made from grapes.

did you know?

window

From its origin, a *window* is a 'wind-eye' – it is an opening like an eye that lets in the air or the wind. It comes from two old Norse words, *vindr*, meaning 'wind' and *auga*, meaning 'eye'.

wing NOUN **1** one of the two parts on the sides of a bird's body that it uses to fly. **2** one of the two parts on the sides of an aeroplane that help it to fly. **3** one of the parts of a car covering the wheels. **4** the position of a player in games like football.

winter NOUN the season of the year that comes after autumn and before spring.

winter

wipe VERB (wiping, wiped) to clean or dry the surface of something by lightly rubbing it.

wire NOUN a thin thread of metal.

wish NOUN a desire or longing for something.

wish VERB to want something to be true, to want to do something.

with 1 having. *A girl with blue eyes.* **2** in the company of, including. *They came with us.* **3** using. *He walked with a stick.* **4** because of. *The chimney was black with soot.*

without not having.

wolf

wives *See* **wife**.

woke, woken *See* **wake**. *I woke up late.*

wolf NOUN (PLURAL wolves) a wild animal like a large dog.

wolves *See* **wolf**.

woman NOUN (PLURAL women) an adult female.

women *See* **woman**.

won *See* **win**. *Our team won the game.*

won't = will not. *I won't go.*

wonder NOUN a feeling of surprise and amazement or the cause of this feeling.

wonder VERB **1** to be surprised and amazed. **2** to want to know or understand.

wonderful ADJECTIVE very good and pleasing.

wood NOUN **1** the material that tree trunks and branches are made of. **2** a place where trees grow together.

woodpecker NOUN a bird with a long, sharp beak for boring holes in tree trunks to eat insects.

wool NOUN **1** the soft, thick hair that grows on sheep, goats, etc. **2** the thread or material made from this hair.

word NOUN the letters and sounds that together make up a single unit of language.

wore *See* **wear**. *Sarah wore a new dress.*

work VERB **1** to do a task, especially as a job. **2** to move or go properly. *He got the engine to work at last.*

work NOUN a job, a task.

worm NOUN a long, thin creature without legs that lives in the soil.

worn *See* **wear**. *He had worn his new T-shirt to the party.*

worse ADJECTIVE *See* **bad**. *Even worse news.*

worst ADJECTIVE *See* **bad**. *The worst winter for years.*

would used in reported speech or writing, to express a condition, etc. *You said you would come.*

wouldn't = would not. *I wouldn't say that.*

wrinkle NOUN a line in your skin, especially when you grow old.

Xx

Xmas NOUN a short way of writing 'Christmas'.

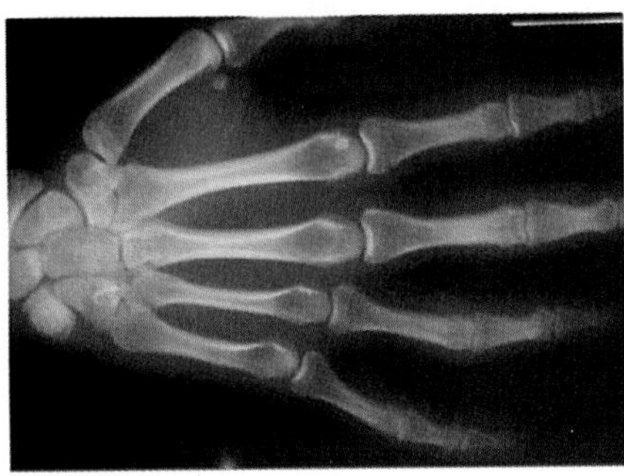

X-ray

X-ray NOUN **1** a beam of radiation that takes pictures of the inside of your body. **2** the picture made by sending X-rays through your body.

xylophone NOUN a musical instrument that you play by hitting flat bars with a hammer.

---

yacht NOUN a sailing boat.

yarn NOUN thread.

yawn VERB to open your mouth wide, as when you are tired or bored.

yo-yo

Yy

year NOUN a period of time equal to 365 days, 52 weeks or 12 months.

yell VERB to shout out.

yellow ADJECTIVE having the colour of egg yolks.

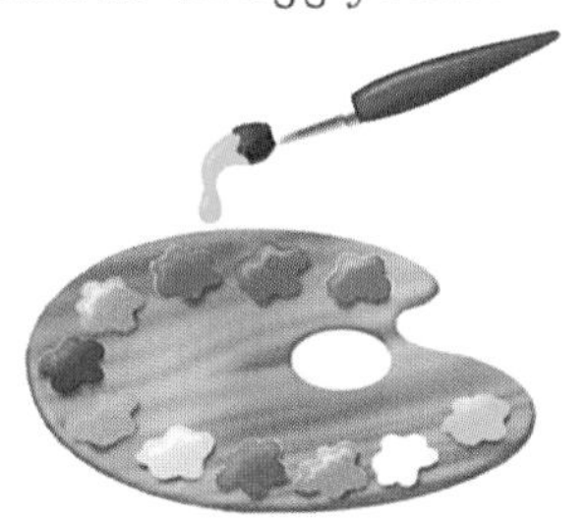

yellow

yes used to answer someone to agree with them, or to say that something is true.

yesterday the day before today.

yet up to this time.

yo-yo NOUN a toy made of a round piece of wood or plastic on a string that you make go up and down.

yogurt NOUN food made from milk.

yolk NOUN the yellow part in the middle of an egg.

you (yourself, yourselves) the person or people being spoken to. *Would you like to come with me?*

you'd = you had, you would. *You'd know them.*

you'll = you will. *You'll be sorry.*

Zz

you're = you are. *You're lucky.*

you've = you have. *You've been told.*

young ADJECTIVE not old.

your belonging to you.

yours that or those belonging to you.

yourself, yourselves *See* **you**. *Did you enjoy yourself last night?*

zebra

zebra NOUN wild animal like a horse, with black and white stripes.

zero NOUN the figure 0, nothing.

zig-zag NOUN a line shaped like a row of Ws.

zip NOUN a fastener with two rows of teeth which you pull together to fasten things.

zoo NOUN a park where wild animals are kept in cages for people to look at.

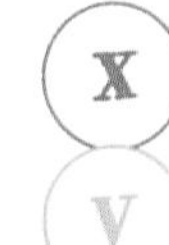

Adjectives, nouns and verbs

Adjectives

An **adjective** is a word that tells us about a noun. *In 'a small car' 'small' is an adjective that describes 'car'.*

When we compare two people or things, we add *–er* to the adjective or put *more* in front of the adjective: *rich, richer; small, smaller; more dangerous.*

When we compare three or more people or things we add *–est* to the adjective or put *most* in front of the adjective: *rich, richest; small, smallest; most dangerous.*

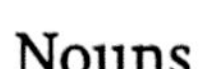

Nouns

The name of a thing is called a **noun**. There are different kinds of noun.

A **proper noun** is the name of a particular person or thing. Your name is a proper noun. The names of places are also proper nouns. Examples of proper nouns are: *William Shakespeare, France, London, Queen Elizabeth.* Proper nouns start with a capital letter.
All other nouns are called *common nouns*, for example: *book, child, rice.*

Concrete nouns are the names given to things that you can see or touch, for example: *book, child, dog.*

Ee Ff Gg Hh

Abstract nouns are the names given to feelings, qualities or ideas, for example: *surprise, happiness, beauty.*

Collective nouns are the names of a group of people or things. For example: 'flock' in 'a flock of sheep'; 'crowd' in 'a crowd of people'.

The **singular** is the form of a noun that we use when we talk about one person or thing. This is in contrast to the **plural**, the form of a noun that we use when we talk about two or more people or things.
For example, the plural of 'dog' is 'dogs'. The most common way to make a word into the plural is to add 's': *book, books.*

Verbs
A **verb** is a 'doing' word. It tells us what is happening or being. Examples of verbs are: *go, think, play*.

A verb shows us when an action takes place. For example with the verb 'help':

present I help; I am helping
past I helped; I have helped
future I will help

The spelling of the verb changes when the word is used to show different times. For example, 'ed' is usually added when the verb is used in the past: *help, helped (I helped Dad yesterday).*

Ii Jj Kk Ll Mm

Qq Pp Oo Nn

a b c d e f g h i j k l m n o p q r s t u v w x y z

Acknowledgements

The publishers would like to thank the following artists who have contributed to this book:

David Ashby (Illustration Ltd.), Andrew Clark, Wayne Ford, Mike Foster (Maltings Partnership), Jeremy Gower, Kuo Kang Chen, Martin Sanders, Mike Saunders, Guy Smith, Mike White (Temple Rogers).

Commissioned photography by Pat Spillane (Creative Vision).

All other photographs from Miles Kelly archives.